Case Studies in Islamic Banking and Finance

Case Questions & Answers

Brian Kettell

A John Wiley and Sons, Ltd., Publication

This edition first published in 2011
© 2011 Brian Kettell

Registered office
John Wiley & Sons Ltd, The Atrium, Southern Gate, Chichester, West Sussex, PO19 8SQ, United Kingdom

For details of our global editorial offices, for customer services and for information about how to apply for permission to reuse the copyright material in this book please see our website at www.wiley.com.

ISBN 978-0-470-97801-6 (paperback)
ISBN 978-1-119-99056-7 (ebook)
ISBN 978-1-119-99057-4 (ebook)
ISBN 978-1-119-99128-1 (ebook)

A catalogue record for this book is available from the British Library.

Typeset in 10/12pt Times by Aptara Inc., New Delhi, India

Printed in Great Britain by CPI Antony Rowe, Chippenham, Wiltshire

To my wife Nadia, our son Alexei and daughter Anna.
Nadia keeps the whole fleet on an even keel with only the
occasional shipwreck.

Case Studies in Islamic
Banking and Finance

For other titles in the Wiley Finance series
please see www.wiley.com/finance

Contents

Preface

The Islamic finance industry is in the midst of a phenomenal expansionary phase, exhibiting average annual growth rates of about 15 per cent in recent years. This rapid growth has been fuelled not only by surging demand for *Sharia'a* compliant products from financiers from the Middle East and other Muslim countries, but also by investors around the world, thus rendering the expansion of Islamic finance a global phenomenon. Besides its wide geographical scope, the rapid expansion of Islamic finance is also taking place across the whole spectrum of financial activities, ranging from retail banking to insurance and capital market investments.

Educational and training material for the Islamic banking and finance industry is, however, lagging far behind the speed at which the industry is evolving. Indeed the lack of quality educational and training material has now become a serious obstacle to effective training and education. This book, the **first ever case study book on Islamic banking and finance**, is designed to enable students and practitioners to test their understanding of the underlying principles. Emphasis is placed on case studies and tests of the basic concepts. Suggested answers are provided.

The case study method was pioneered at Harvard Law School. A case study is expected to capture the complexity of a single case, and the methodology which enables this has developed within the social sciences. Such methodology is applied not only in the social sciences, such as psychology, sociology, anthropology, and economics, but also in practice-oriented fields such as environmental studies, social work, education, and business studies but has, until now, not been available to the Islamic finance industry.

WHAT IS A CASE STUDY?

A case study is a description of an actual business situation involving a decision to be made or a problem to be solved. It can be a real situation that actually happened just as described or where portions have been disguised for reasons of privacy. Most case studies are written in such a way that the reader takes the place of the manager whose responsibility is to make decisions to help solve the problem. In almost all case studies, a decision must be made, although that decision might be to leave the situation as it is and do nothing.

A case study is a research methodology common in social science. It is based on an in-depth investigation of a single individual, group, or event. Case studies may be descriptive or explanatory. The latter type is used to explore causation in order to find underlying principles. Rather than using samples and following a rigid protocol (strict set of rules) to examine a limited number of variables, case study methods involve an in-depth, longitudinal (over a long period of time) examination of a single instance or event: a **case**. They provide a systematic way of looking at events, collecting data, analysing information, and reporting the results. As a result the researcher may gain a sharpened understanding of why the instance happened as it did, and what might become important to look at more extensively in future research. Case studies lend themselves to both generating and testing hypotheses.

THE CASE METHOD AS A LEARNING TOOL

The *case method of analysis* is a learning tool in which students and Instructors participate in direct discussion of case studies, as opposed to the lecture method, where the Instructor speaks and students listen and take notes. In the case method, students teach themselves, with the Instructor being an active guide, rather than just a talking head delivering content. The focus is on students learning through their joint, co-operative effort.

Assigned cases are first prepared by students, and this preparation forms the basis for class discussion under the direction of the Instructor. Students learn, often unconsciously, how to evaluate a problem, how to make decisions, and how to orally argue a point of view. Using this method, they also learn how to think in terms of the problems faced. In courses that use the case method extensively, a significant part of the student's evaluation may rest with classroom participation in case discussions, with another substantial portion resting on written case analyses. For these reasons, using the case method tends to be very intensive for both students and Instructor.

HOW TO DO A CASE STUDY

While there is no one definitive "Case Method" or approach, there are common steps that most approaches recommend are followed in tackling a case study. It is inevitable that different Instructors will do things differently; this is part of life and will also be part of working for others. This variety is beneficial since it will show participants different ways of approaching decision making.

Instructors seeking to apply the case study methodology should follow an organised format as discussed below.

Beforehand (usually a week before), the participants get:

1. the case study,
2. (often) some guiding questions that will need to be answered, and
3. (sometimes) some reading assignments that have some relevance to the case subject.

Participants then work in completing the case and the procedure can be divided up into three components:

1. what participants need to do to prepare before the class discussion,
2. what takes place in the class discussion of the case, and
3. anything required after the class discussion has taken place.

For maximum effectiveness, it is essential that the instructor manages all three components.

It must be stressed that the newness of the industry means that designing quality educational and training material is fraught with problems, particularly with case studies. In addition to this newness the industry also faces the challenge of changing *Sharia'a* interpretations of many of the products. In addition the existence of different schools of Islamic jurisprudence (*Fiqh*) combined with controversies revolving around *sukuk* (Islamic bonds) has certainly created some uncertainties as to how the contracts are being applied. Recent high profile court cases have also created uncertainties about the applications of some of the contracts.

These factors lead to the potential for controversy over some of my suggested case answers. No doubt some of the answers will be disputed. I cannot claim to have universal answers and would ask that readers please assume that these may change over time.

If readers do feel strongly that they have an alternative case answer I would certainly welcome a dialogue. Indeed if anyone wishes to provide me with reasons for their proposed alternative solutions I would urge them to please do so. It is this dialogue which is so important for the health and future of the industry and I look forward to an active debate with the readers. My email is brian.kettell@islamicbankingcourses.com

No answers to Case Studies 8 and 10 are provided. In one case it involves an Excel spreadsheet which should be simple to set up and the second case has the answers within the case itself.

Companion texts, *Introduction to Islamic Banking and Finance* **and** *The Islamic Banking and Finance Workbook* **are available from the publishers.**

Introduction

WHAT ARE THE PRINCIPLES OF ISLAMIC BANKING AND FINANCE?

Islamic financial institutions are those that are based, in their objectives and operations, on *Qur'anic* principles. They are thus set apart from 'conventional' institutions, which have no such religious preoccupations. Islamic banks provide commercial services that comply with the religious injunctions of Islam. Crucially, these banks provide services to their customers free from interest, (the Arabic term for which is *riba*), and the giving and taking of interest is prohibited in all transactions. This prohibition makes an Islamic banking system differ fundamentally from a conventional banking system.

Technically, *riba* refers to the addition in the amount of the principal of a loan according to the time for which it is loaned and the amount of the loan. In earlier, historical times there was a fierce debate as to whether the term *riba* relates to interest or usury, although there now appears to be consensus of opinion among Islamic scholars that the term extends to all forms of interest.

In Islamic law (the *Sharia'a*), *riba* means an addition, however slight, over and above the principal. According to the Federal *Sharia'a* Court of Pakistan the concept covers both usury and interest; is not restricted to doubled and redoubled interest; applies to all forms of interest, whether large or small, simple or compound, doubled or redoubled; and the Islamic injunction is not only against exorbitant or excessive interest, but also against even a minimal rate of interest. Financial systems based on Islamic tenets are therefore dedicated to the elimination of the payment and receipt of interest in all forms, and this taboo makes Islamic banks and other financial institutions different in principle from their conventional counterparts.

There is a range of modern interpretations of why *riba* is considered *haram* (forbidden) but these are strictly secondary to the religious underpinnings.

The fundamental sources of Islam are the Holy *Qur'an* and the *Sunnah*, a term that in Ancient Arabia meant 'ancestral precedent' or the 'custom of the tribe', but which is now synonymous with the teachings and traditions of the Prophet Mohammed as transmitted by the relaters of authentic tradition. Both of these sources treat interest as an act of exploitation and injustice and as such it is inconsistent with Islamic notions of fairness and property rights. Although it is often claimed that there is more than this to Islamic banking, such as its contribution towards economic development and a more equitable distribution of income and wealth, its increased equity participation in the economy and so on, Islamic banking nevertheless derives its specific *raison d'être* from the fact that there is no place for the institution of interest in the Islamic order.

This rejection of interest poses the central question of what replaces the interest rate mechanism in an Islamic framework. Financial intermediation is at the heart of modern financial systems. If the paying and receiving of interest is prohibited, how do Islamic banks operate? Here profit and loss sharing (PLS) comes in as a substitute for interest as a method of resource allocation and financial intermediation.

In fact, the basic idea of Islamic banking can be stated simply. The operations of Islamic financial institutions primarily are based on a PLS principle. An Islamic bank does not charge interest but rather participates in the yield resulting from the use of funds. The depositors also share in the profits of the bank according to a predetermined ratio. There is thus a partnership between the Islamic bank and its depositors, on one side, and between the bank and its investment clients, on the other side, as a manager of depositors' resources in productive uses.

This is in contrast with a conventional bank, which mainly borrows funds, paying interest on one side of the balance sheet, and lends funds, charging interest on the other. The complexity of Islamic banking comes from the variety (and nomenclature) of the instruments employed, and in understanding the underpinnings of Islamic law.

Six key principles drive the activities of Islamic banks:

- the prohibition of predetermined loan repayments as interest (*riba*);
- risk sharing is at the heart of the Islamic system;
- making money out of money is unacceptable – all financial transactions must be asset-backed;
- prohibition of speculative behaviour;
- only *Sharia'a* approved contracts are acceptable;
- the sanctity of contracts.

The principles as applied to Islamic banking and finance are set out below in the following sections.

Predetermined Payments are Prohibited

Any predetermined payment over and above the actual amount of principal is prohibited. Islam allows only one kind of loan and that is *qard al hassan* (literally 'good loan'), whereby the lender does not charge any interest or additional amount over the money lent.

Traditional Muslim Jurists have construed this principle so strictly that, according to one Islamic scholar, 'the prohibition applies to any advantage or benefits that the lender might secure out of the *qard* (loan) such as riding the borrower's mule, eating at his table or even taking advantage of the shade of his wall'. The principle derived from the quotation emphasises that any associated or indirect benefits that could potentially accrue to the lender are also prohibited.

Profit and Loss Sharing

The principle here is that the lender must share in the profits or losses arising out of the enterprise for which the money was lent. Islam encourages Muslims to invest their money and to become partners in order to share profits and risks in the business instead of becoming creditors. Islamic finance is based on the belief that the provider of capital and the user of capital should equally share the risk of business ventures, whether those are manufacturing industries, service sector companies or simple trade deals. Translated into banking terms, the depositor, the bank and the borrower should all share the risks and the rewards of financing business ventures.

This is unlike the interest-based conventional banking system, where all the pressure is on the borrower: he must pay back his loan, with the agreed interest, regardless of the success or failure of his venture.

The principle, which thereby emerges, is that in order to try and ensure investments are made into productive enterprises Islam encourages these types of investments in order that the community may ultimately benefit. However, Islam is not willing to allow a loophole to exist for those who do not wish to invest and take risks, but are instead intent on hoarding money or depositing money in a bank in return for receiving interest (*riba*) on these funds for no risk (other than the bank becoming insolvent).

Accordingly, under Islam, either people invest with risk or suffer loss by keeping their money idle. Islam encourages the notion of higher risks and higher returns and promotes it by leaving no other avenue available to investors. The objective here is that high-risk investments provide a stimulus to the economy and encourage entrepreneurs to maximise their efforts to make them succeed.

Risk Sharing

As mentioned one of the most important feature of Islamic banking is that it promotes risk sharing between the providers of funds (investors) and the user of funds (entrepreneur). By contrast, under conventional banking, the investor is assured of a predetermined rate of interest. Since the nature of this world is uncertain, the results of any project are not known with certainty *ex ante*, and so there is always some risk involved.

In conventional banking, all this risk is borne by the entrepreneur. Whether the project succeeds and produces a profit or fails and produces a loss, the owner of capital is still rewarded with a predetermined return. In Islam, this kind of unjust distribution is not allowed. In Islamic banking both the investor and the entrepreneur share the results of the project in an equitable way. In the case of profit, both share this in pre-agreed proportions. In the case of loss, all financial loss is borne by the capital supplier with the entrepreneur being penalised by receiving no return (wages or salary) for his endeavours.

Emphasis on Productivity as Compared to Credit-worthiness

Under conventional banking, almost all that matters to a bank is that its loan and the interest thereon are paid on time. Therefore, in granting loans, the dominant consideration is the credit-worthiness of the borrower. Under PLS banking, the bank will receive a return only if the project succeeds and produces a profit. Therefore, it is reasoned, an Islamic bank will be more concerned with the soundness of the project and the business acumen and managerial competence of the entrepreneur.

Making Money out of Money is not Acceptable

Making money from money is not Islamically acceptable. Money, in Islam, is only a medium of exchange, a way of defining the value of a thing. It has no value in itself, and therefore should not be allowed to generate more money, via fixed interest payments, simply by being put in a bank or lent to someone else.

The human effort, initiative and risk involved in a productive venture are more important than the money used to finance it. Muslim Jurists consider money as potential capital rather than capital, meaning that money becomes capital only when it is invested in business. Accordingly, money advanced to a business as a loan is regarded as a debt of the business and not capital; as such, it is not entitled to any return (i.e., interest).

Muslims are encouraged to spend and/or invest in productive investments and are discouraged from keeping money idle. Hoarding money is regarded as being Islamically unacceptable. In Islam, money represents purchasing power, which is considered to be the only proper use of money. This purchasing power (money) cannot be used to make more purchasing power (money) without undergoing the intermediate step of it being used for the purchase of goods and services.

Uncertainty is Prohibited

Gharar (uncertainty, risk or speculation) is also prohibited, and so any financial transaction entered into should be free from these aspects.

Contracting parties should have perfect knowledge of the counter values (goods received and/or prices paid) intended to be exchanged as a result of their transactions. Also, parties cannot predetermine a guaranteed profit. This is based on the principle of 'uncertain gains', which on a strict interpretation does not even allow an undertaking from the customer to repay the borrowed principal plus an amount to take into account inflation. The rationale behind the prohibition is the wish to protect the weak from exploitation. Therefore, options and futures are considered as un-Islamic and so are forward foreign exchange transactions, given that forward rates are determined by interest rate differentials.

Only *Sharia'a*-approved Contracts are Acceptable

Conventional banking is secular in its orientation. In contrast, in the Islamic system, all economic agents have to work within the moral value system of Islam. Islamic banks are no exception. As such, they cannot finance any project that conflicts with the moral value system of Islam. For example, Islamic banks are not allowed to finance a distillery, a casino, a night club or any other activity prohibited by Islam or known to be harmful to society.

Sanctity of Contracts

Many verses in the Holy *Qur'an* encourage trade and commerce, and the attitude of Islam is that there should be no impediment to honest and legitimate trade and business, in order that people earn a living, support their families and give charity to those less fortunate.

Just as Islam regulates and influences all other spheres of life, so it also governs the conduct of business and commerce. Muslims have a moral obligation to conduct their business activities in accordance with the requirements of their religion. They should be fair, honest and just towards others. A special obligation exists upon vendors because there is no doctrine of *caveat emptor* in Islam. Monopolies and price-fixing are prohibited.

The basic principles of the law are laid down in the four root transactions of (1) sales (*bay*), transfer of the ownership or corpus of property for a consideration; (2) hire (*Ijara*), transfer of the usufruct (right to use) of property for a consideration; (3) gift (*hiba*), gratuitous transfer of the corpus of property; and (4) loan (*ariyah*), gratuitous transfer of the usufruct of property.

These basic principles are then applied to the various specific transactions of, for example, pledge, deposit, guarantee, agency, assignment, land tenancy, *waqf* foundations (religious or charitable bodies) and partnerships.

Islam upholds contractual obligations and the disclosure of information as a sacred duty. This feature is intended to reduce the risk of asymmetric information and moral hazard, potentially major problems for Islamic banks.

About the Author

Brian Kettell has a wealth of practical experience in the area of Islamic banking and finance. He worked for several years as an Advisor for the Central Bank of Bahrain where he had numerous Islamic banking responsibilities.

Subsequently, Brian taught courses on Islamic banking and finance at a range of financial institutions including the World Bank, National Commercial Bank (Saudi Arabia), Global Investment House (Kuwait), Noor Islamic Bank (UAE), the UK Treasury, the Central Bank of Iran, the Central Bank of Syria, the Chartered Institute for Securities and Investment, the Institute for Financial Services and Scotland Yard.

Brian's vast academic expertise in Islamic finance is highlighted by his role as former Joint Editor of the *Islamic Finance Qualification Handbook* and his past teaching work at a number of top universities worldwide including the London School of Economics, the City University of Hong Kong, the American University of the Middle East in Kuwait and London Metropolitan University Business School.

Brian's impressive list of publications include over 100 articles in journals, business magazines and the financial press including *Islamic Business and Finance, Islamic Banking and Finance*, the *Central Banking Journal, Euromoney*, the *Securities Journal and the International Currency Review*. He has also published 16 books on Islamic banking and financial markets.

1

Case Study 1: *Ijara* Contract

1.1 LEARNING OUTCOMES

After working through Case Study 1 you should be able to do the following:

- Define the *Ijara* contract.
- Define the *Ijara wa Iqtina* contract.
- Distinguish a conventional loan from *Ijara*.
- Describe the elements of an *Ijara* transaction.
- Contrast *Ijara* with the other modes of Islamic finance.
- Identify the reasoning behind the *Sharia'a* rulings on *Ijara*.
- Describe the different forms of *Ijara*.
- Explain the practicalities of implementing *Ijara*.
- Identify the Arabic terminology used in *Ijara*.
- Describe the *Sharia'a* rulings on *Ijara*.
- Contrast conventional leasing with Islamic leasing.
- Explain the role that interest can play within an *Ijara* transaction.
- Identify problems associated with applying *Ijara*.
- Explain the importance of deferred sales within Islamic finance.
- Contrast the role of penalty defaults within conventional and Islamic finance.
- Explain how *Ijara* can be used for home finance.
- Define LIBOR and explain its application with an *Ijara* contract.
- Identify the deferred sale versus profit and loss share contracts.
- Test that you have fully understood the principles that underlie the *Ijara* contract.

1.2 ROLE OF *IJARA* IN ISLAMIC FINANCE

> Those who take *riba* (usury or interest) will not stand but as stands the one whom the demon has driven crazy by his touch.
>
> *Qur'an Sura 2: 275–280*

Case Abstract

Ijara is an Arabic term, with origins in Islamic *Fiqh*, meaning to give something to rent. Leasing is a contract whereby usufruct rights to an asset are transferred by the owner, known as the lessor, to another person, known as the lessee, at an agreed-upon price, called the rent, and for an agreed-upon period of time, called the term of the lease. This case study describes the rationale and application of the *Ijara* financing technique. The example provided is that of car finance but it could have equally will have been applied to any physical capital asset used in business.

1.3 THE *IJARA* CONTRACT AS A MODE OF ISLAMIC FINANCE

1.3.1 What is The *Ijara* Contract?

Ijara is an Islamic mode of finance adopted by Islamic banks. *Ijara* (leasing) is a medium to long-term method of financing capital equipment or property. Under this contract, the customer selects the capital equipment or property (assets) to be financed by the bank and the bank then purchases these assets from the manufacturer or supplier and then leases them to the customer for an agreed period.

In conformity with the *Sharia'a*, the owner of the assets (in this case the bank) must be paid rent (fixed or variable, as agreed by the lessor and lessee) and must exercise all the rights and obligations that are incidental to ownership such as maintaining, insuring and repairing the assets.

The lessee, on the other hand, obtains the use of the asset for the period of the lease subject to paying the rent. The lessee may assume the obligations, such as maintaining, insuring and repairing the asset, in return for a reduced rent.

1.3.2 What is Car *Ijara*?

As mentioned above *Ijara* is basically the transfer of usufruct (defined below) of a fixed asset to another person for an agreed period, for an agreed consideration. Under a Car *Ijara* agreement the car will be rented to the customer for the period agreed at the time of contract. Upon completion of the lease period the customer in the Meezan case discussed below, gets ownership of the car against his initial security deposit.

Car *Ijara* is a *Sharia'a*-compliant car-leasing scheme. It is based on the principles of *Ijara* and is completely free from the element of interest. This product is designed for interest-averse individuals, looking for a car-financing scheme that helps in avoiding interest-based transactions. So Car *Ijara* is simply a rental agreement under which the car will be given to the customer in exchange for rent for a period, agreed at the time of the contract.

Meezan Bank, based in Pakistan and a pioneer in this area, purchases the car and rents it out to the customer for a period of three, four or five years. Upon completion of the lease period the customer gets ownership of the car against his initial security deposit.

Somewhat confusingly, the Meezan Car *Ijara* scheme has elements of *Ijara wa Iqtina* within it. In this case study I propose to follow the Meezan assumption in using *Ijara* in the sense that it involves car ownership at the end of the maturity of the deal. This is in line with *Sharia'a* methodology and terminology.

1.3.2.1 What is Usufruct?

Usufruct is the right of enjoying a thing, the property of which is vested in another, and to draw from the same all the profit, utility and advantage that it may produce, provided it be without altering the substance of the thing. Items without usufruct cannot be leased. It is necessary for a valid lease contract that the corpus of the leased asset remains in the ownership of the seller, and only its usufruct is transferred to the lessee.

1.3.3 In what Sense is Car *Ijara* Interest Free?

In Car *Ijara*, the asset remains under the ownership and at the risk of the bank and the customer only pays the rental for the use of the asset, just like the rent of a house.

Under leasing or lease purchase, the Islamic financial institution buys the financed asset and retains the title through the life of the contract. The customer makes a series of lease payments over a specified period of time, and may have the option at the end to buy the item from the lessor (and owner) at a pre specified residual value.

Leasing was not originally a mode of financing. It was simply a transaction meant to transfer the usufruct of a property from one person to another for an agreed period and an agreed upon consideration. Leasing can be used as a mode of financing, in Islamic banks, as an alternative to conventional car financing. However, the consideration of leasing as a mode of financing should be based on certain conditions. It should be understood, by all using it as a mode of financing, that it is not sufficient to substitute the term 'interest' with the term 'rent', and use the term 'mortgage' instead of the term 'leased asset'. There must be a significant difference between leasing and an interest-bearing loan.

It is no secret that an Islamic bank or financial institution will take into consideration the same factors as a conventional bank when determining the rental payments and residual value. These would include the rate of inflation, the creditworthiness of the lessee, the opportunity cost value of the money (as reflected by market interest rates) and so on. An implicit 'interest rate' can trivially be calculated from the price, residual value, term of the lease and the lease payment. This fact is not hidden. Indeed Muslim customers are encouraged to 'shop around' and ensure that the Islamic financial institution is not implicitly charging an interest rate, which is in line with the conventional market.

In the final analysis, however, the difference is in the form of the contract. If the lease is structured in accordance with the various conditions within Islamic jurisprudence, it will contract no *riba* and ensure that it cannot contain such forbidden *riba* in the future (e. g., in terms of late payment fees, etc.).

1.3.4 What is the Difference between a Conventional Lease and an Islamic Lease?

The most important financial difference between Islamic leasing and conventional leasing is that, with Islamic leasing, the leasing agency must own the leased object for the duration of the lease. Therefore, although leasing a car from a car manufacturer or car dealership may in principle be permitted for Muslims (if the contract satisfies the other conditions), Muslims should investigate further. In many cases, the car dealership may in fact use a bank or other financial intermediary to provide a loan for the present value of lease payments, and charge the customer interest on this loan. This would constitute the forbidden *riba*.

Scrupulous Islamic financial institutions ensure that the contract abides by all the restrictions set out in the *Sharia'a* (e. g., subleasing requires the permission of the lessor; late payment penalties must be handled very carefully to avoid *riba*, etc.).

The differences between conventional and Islamic financing schemes are described in the sections below.

1.3.4.1 *Leasing versus Conventional Financing*

Conventional Financing

The conventional financing schemes provide financing for purchasing a car; that is, in essence the financier is giving a loan and charging interest.

Islamic Financing

The Islamic car financing – *Ijara* – is based on a lease contract. It is not a financing scheme; rather it is a lease contract. As mentioned earlier leasing is a contract whereby usufruct rights to an asset are transferred by the owner, known as the lessor, to another person, known as the lessee, at an agreed-upon price, called the rent, and for an agreed-upon period of time, called the term of lease.

1.3.4.2 Rentals versus Instalments

Conventional Financing

A conventional car financing scheme is actually an interest-based loan given by the financial institution, with interest being charged on the loan.

Islamic Financing

Islamic car financing is based on pure rentals. In Car *Ijara* the asset remains at the ownership and risk of the bank and the customer only pays the rental for use of the asset, just like the rent for a house.

1.3.4.3 Ownership

Conventional Financing

In conventional car financing, the car is purchased in the name of the buyer from the dealer.

Islamic Financing

Under *Ijara* the ownership remains with the bank; that is, the car is purchased from the dealer in the name of the bank. This is because it is one of the foremost conditions of the Islamic mode of leasing that an object cannot be leased out unless it is in the possession of the lessor.

1.3.4.4 Risk/loss

Conventional Financing

Since the car is bought in the name of the buyer in the traditional mode of car financing, the risk is immediately transferred to the buyer, whereas in the case of Islamic financing, this is not so.

Islamic Financing

The car is purchased in the name of the bank from the dealer and so the risk remains entirely with the bank. As the corpus of the leased property remains in the ownership of the lessor, all the liabilities and risks emerging from the ownership are borne by the lessor.

The lessee is responsible for any loss caused to the asset by misuse or negligence. The lessee can also be made liable for the wear and tear, which normally occurs during its use. But the lessee cannot be made liable for a loss caused by factors beyond his control. (The agreements with traditional car financing generally do not differentiate between these two situations.) In a lease based on Islamic principles, both situations should be dealt with separately.

1.3.4.5   Down-Payment versus Security Deposit

Conventional Financing

Both the down-payment and the security deposit are one-time payments. The major difference occurs because the buyer can buy back the car against the security deposit in the case of *Ijara*, whereas in conventional banking the down-payment remains with the bank, and no buy-back of the car can occur against the down-payment.

Islamic Financing

With *Ijara* the buyer is required to keep a security deposit at the bank. There is a minimum and a maximum requirement for the security deposit. The requirement is different in the case of conventional car financing, where a down-payment is made by the buyer of the car.

1.3.4.6   Return of the Car

Conventional Financing

In a traditional car financing scheme, the customer takes out a loan to purchase the car, which he cannot return under any circumstances whatsoever, unless he pays off the loan.

Islamic Financing

In the Islamic mode of financing, the buyer has the right to return the car anytime during or at the end of the lease period. Since this is a lease agreement, and the lessee has been paying rentals, he can return the car to the bank and take back the security deposit any time he wishes.

1.3.4.7   Termination of Contract

The buyer of the car has the option and right to terminate the contract and return the car before the contract reaches its maturity in both the conventional and Islamic mode of car financing. The difference lies in the post-termination phase.

Conventional Financing

In the conventional car financing scheme, if the customer wants to terminate the contract the only option he has is to buy the car by paying the rest of the instalments.

Islamic Financing

In the Islamic car financing scheme, the customer has two options: either return the car and get back the security deposit or buy the car from the bank at the market value plus a certain percentage of spread for the bank.

1.3.4.8 Documentation Differences

Sequence/process

Islam considers the procedure in which any transaction takes place as a significant factor in all modes of financing. The underlying difference between the Islamic and conventional modes of financing is that of the process. To Muslims, not only the end result but also the means to it are important.

If the result is correct and the steps are wrong, or vice versa, the entire process is deemed invalid, from a *Sharia'a* perspective. According to *Sharia'a* principles, lawful steps to lawful results are very important.

The most important financial difference between Islamic permitted leasing and conventional financial leasing is that the leasing agency must own the leased object for the duration of the lease. Ownership of the asset is the prerequisite for leasing out its usufruct. As mentioned, Islam places great emphasis on the sequencing.

1.3.5 The Meezan Bank Car *Ijara* Scheme

Meezan Bank's Car *Ijara* has been designed according to the principles of Islam and is completely interest-free. Moreover the *Ijara* contract and other documentation also comply with *Sharia'a* requirements. In contrast, a conventional car-financing scheme is actually an interest-based loan given by the financial institution with interest being charged on the loan. Also, in conventional car-leasing schemes, the lease contract is not in compliance with *Sharia'a* law and has *riba* and other un-Islamic elements in it.

1.3.5.1 What Makes Car **Ijara** Unique?

Some of the key characteristics of the Meezan Car *Ijara* are described in the following sections.

Rights and Liabilities of Owner Versus User

Ijara is an asset-based contract, that is, the lessor should have ownership of the asset during the life of the contract. Under *Sharia'a* law all ownership-related rights and liabilities should lie with the owners while all usage-related rights and liabilities should lie with the user.

A conventional lease contract does not distinguish between the nature of these liabilities and dumps all liabilities on the user. This is not permitted under the *Sharia'a*. Under *Ijara* all ownership-related risks lie with the bank and all usage related links lie with the user, thus making the lessor the true owner of the asset and making the income generated through the contract permissible (*halal*) for the Islamic bank.

Continuation of Lease Rentals in the Case of Total Loss or Theft of Vehicle

If the leased vehicle is stolen or completely destroyed the conventional leasing company would continue charging the lease holder rent until the settlement of the insurance claim. Under the Islamic system, however, rent is consideration for usage of the leased asset and, if the asset has been stolen or destroyed, the concept of rental becomes void. As such, in the above-mentioned eventualities, Meezan Bank does not charge the lease rental.

Is there a Penalty for Late Payment of Rent? If so How is This Permissible Under the Sharia'a?

In most conventional financial leases an extra monetary amount is charged if rent is not paid on time. This extra amount is considered as *riba* under the *Sharia'a* and is distinctly forbidden (*haram*). The lessee may be asked to undertake that if he fails to pay rent on its due date, he will pay a certain amount to a charity that will be administered through the bank. For this purpose Meezan Bank maintains a charity fund where such amounts may be credited and disbursed for charitable purposes.

What is the Insurance Arrangement under Car Ijara?

Being the owner of the car, the bank will be responsible for insurance of the car and for paying the insurance premium. If *Takaful* (Islamic insurance) is not available, the insurance is done under the conventional system.

Can the User Buy the Car Prior to the Termination of Rental Agreement?

Yes. The rental agreement contains the purchase price schedule.

Is the Product Approved by Meezan Bank's Sharia'a Board

Yes. Car *Ijara* is designed under the supervision of Meezan Bank's *Sharia'a* Supervisory Board and is approved by the Board.

In order for any Islamic financing technique to be acceptable to the Islamic community it has to be endorsed by the appropriate *Sharia'a* Board who will provide a *Fatwa* (a religious ruling). The appendix to this case illustrates the *Fatwa* applicable to the Meezan Bank Car *Ijara* agreement.

How do you Calculate the Rent on a New Car?

To calculate the monthly rentals simply multiply the cost of the car with the factors given in Table 1.1.

For example if a customer is interested in a new car costing Rs. 300,000 for a tenure of five years and is willing to pay a 50% security deposit, the monthly rental would be Rs. 300,000 × 0.014067 = Rs. 4220 per month for five years.

What if the Customer Wants to Buy a Second Hand Car?

If a customer is interested in a car costing Rs. 300,000 for a tenure of five years and is willing to pay a 50% security deposit, the monthly rental can be calculated from Table 1.2. The monthly rental would be Rs. 300,000 × 0.014230 = Rs. 4261 per month for five years.

Table 1.3 demonstrates the difference between a Car *Ijara* and a conventional car lease.

Table 1.1   Rental calculation for new cars

Security deposit (%)	3 years	4 years	5 years
15	0.030399	0.024789	0.021590
20	0.028821	0.023533	0.020515
25	0.027242	0.022277	0.019440
30	0.025664	0.021021	0.018366
35	0.024085	0.019765	0.017291
40	0.022507	0.018508	0.016216
45	0.020929	0.017252	0.015142
50	0.019350	0.015996	0.014067

Source: Meezan Bank

Table 1.2   Rental calculation for used cars

Security deposit (%)	3 years	4 years	5 years
20	0.029412	0.023940	0.020726
25	0.027799	0.022660	0.019639
30	0.026186	0.021379	0.018552
35	0.024572	0.020099	0.017465
40	0.022959	0.018819	0.016378
45	0.021346	0.017539	0.015290
50	0.019732	0.016259	0.014230

Source: Meezan Bank

Table 1.3   Difference between Car *Ijara* and a conventional lease

Conventional car leasing systems	Meezan Bank's Car *Ijara*
There are two types of contracts: a financing lease and a loan for car financing. Both of the contracts contain conditions that are not acceptable under the *Sharia'a* Financing leases contain conditions of hire purchase, which is not permissible under the *Sharia'a*. This makes the whole contract void. Car financing under a loan agreement contains conditions of interest. Interest is considered *riba* by the *Sharia'a* and this makes the condition void.	The *Ijara* contract is binding under the *Sharia'a* and does not contain any conditions that make the contract void.
In car financing schemes, the customer is responsible for any kind of loss or damage to the vehicle, irrespective of whether the circumstances are under his control or not. If the insurance company does not compensate for the entire amount, the customer is liable to pay the balance.	All risks pertaining to ownership are borne by the bank. The bank will insure the vehicle and be responsible for any loss or damage to the vehicle caused by circumstances beyond the control of the customer, e. g., theft, loss/damage due to natural disasters like flood, earthquake etc. However, the customer will be responsible for any damage in the event of an accident.

Upfront payments consist of
  Down-payment ranging from 15–20% minimum.
  1st year's insurance premium.
  1st monthly rental instalment.
	A minimum of 20% deposit along with actual documentation and processing costs is paid with no other upfront payment.

Under conventional leasing/financing the vehicle is automatically transferred to the name of the customer.	At the end of the *Ijara* agreement the customer is not obligated to purchase the vehicle. Meezan Bank will make an offer to the customer to invite them to purchase the vehicle at the security deposit price. If the customer wants to receive his deposit back he may do so by returning the car to the bank.

Source: Meezan Bank

1.4 APPENDIX: *IJARA FATWA*

Meezan Bank

Car *Ijara*

Meezan Bank's Car *Ijara* is based on the Islamic principles of *Ijara*. This scheme has the following features:

- Meezan Bank's Car *Ijara* has been structured to comply with the tenets of *Sharia'a* and has been developed in consultation with our *Sharia'a* Advisor, Dr Muhammad Imran Usmani. All the principles and rules pertaining to *Ijara* Agreements are strictly adhered to. It is therefore, an *Ijara* facility which is free of *Riba*.
- Original shareholders and Investors' money will be used in the Car *Ijara* business of the bank.
- Car *Ijara* is available in different tenors.
- Meezan Bank may take a security deposit from the customer at the inception of the *Ijara*.
- The customer will pay monthly rentals for use of the car obtained under the *Ijara* scheme.
- All risks and rewards of ownership of assets will be vested in Meezan Bank.
- All expenses of normal wear and tear will be borne by the customer.
- Rentals under the scheme will be calculated such as to keep them in line with the leasing market.
- The customer will undertake unilaterally that in case of early termination he will buy the asset at the particular price mentioned in that undertaking.
- Meezan Bank will use the Agreement to Lease and Lease Agreement, which is approved by its Supervisory Board.

'... Resolved that the modus operandi defined above for Car *Ijara* is according to the dictate *Sharia'a* ...'

(Signed) _____
Justice (Retired) Muhammad Taqi Usmani

(Signed) _____
Dr Abdul Sattar Abu Ghuddah

(Signed) _____
Dr Muhammad Imran Usmani

1.5 CASE STUDY QUESTIONS

1. Outline the key differences between conventional leasing and Islamic leasing.

_____

_____

_____

_____

2. How do insurance needs differ under conventional leasing and Islamic leasing?

3. What are the key *Sharia'a* requirements for the *Ijara* contract?

4. Would a Car *Ijara* be structured identically to a home purchase *Ijara*?

5. Would non-Muslims consider Car *Ijara* schemes a serious alternative to conventional car finance schemes?

6. Calculate the monthly rental payments when buying a new car, costing Rs. 300,000, for a term of four years, if the potential purchaser is willing to pay a 25% security deposit.

7. Calculate the monthly rental payments when buying a new car, costing Rs. 400,000, for a term of three years, if the potential purchaser is willing to pay a 30% security deposit.

8. Calculate the monthly rental payments when buying a new car, costing Rs. 500,000, for a term of five years, if the potential purchaser is willing to pay a 40% security deposit.

_____

_____

_____

_____

9. Calculate the monthly rental payments when buying a new car, costing Rs. 350,000, for a term of three years, if the potential purchaser is willing to pay a 45% security deposit.

_____

_____

_____

_____

10. Calculate the monthly rental payments when buying a new car, costing Rs. 600,000, for a term of four years, if the potential purchaser is willing to pay a 50% security deposit.

_____

_____

_____

_____

11. Calculate the monthly rental payments when buying a new car, costing Rs. 400,000, for a term of five years, if the potential purchaser is willing to pay a 20% security deposit.

_____

_____

_____

_____

12. Do you think that the *Meezan* Car *Ijara* contract is correctly named?

_____

_____

_____

_____

Case Study 2: *Musharaka* Contract

2.1 LEARNING OUTCOMES

After reading Case Study 2 you should be able to do the following:

- Define the *Musharaka* contract.
- Distinguish a conventional loan from a *Musharaka* contract.
- Describe the elements of a *Musharaka* transaction.
- Contrast *Musharaka* with the other modes of Islamic finance.
- Identify the Arabic terminology used in *Musharaka*.
- Describe the different types of *Musharaka*.
- Identify the reasoning behind the *Sharia'a* rulings on *Musharaka*.
- Explain the practicalities of implementing *Musharaka*.
- Describe the *Sharia'a* rulings on *Musharaka*.
- Identify problems with applying *Musharaka*.
- Explain the importance of deferred sales within Islamic finance.
- Contrast the role of penalty defaults within conventional and Islamic finance.
- Explain how *Musharaka* can be used for home finance.
- Define LIBOR and explain its application with a *Musharaka* contract.
- Identify the deferred sale versus profit and loss share contracts.
- Test that you have fully understood the principles that underlie the *Musharaka* contract.

2.2 ROLE OF *MUSHARAKA* IN ISLAMIC FINANCE

Case Abstract

In conventional banking, 'interest' predetermines a fixed rate of return on a loan advanced by the financier irrespective of the profit earned or loss suffered by the debtor. As interest is deemed impermissible in Islam, the *Musharaka* contract does not envisage a fixed rate of return.

Musharaka is a partnership agreement whereby the Islamic bank provides funds, which are mixed with the funds of the business enterprise and sometimes others. All the providers of capital are entitled to participate in management but are not necessarily required to do so. Any profit is distributed among the partners in pre-agreed ratios, whereas any loss is borne strictly in proportion to respective capital contributions.

This case study describes the rationale and applications of the permanent *Musharaka* contract (Case Study 3 covers the Diminishing *Musharaka* contract.)

2.3 SUMMARY OF *MUSHARAKA*

The literal meaning of the word *Musharaka* is sharing. Under *Sharia'a* law, *Musharaka* refers to a joint partnership whereby two or more persons combine either their capital or labour, forming a business in which all partners share the profit according to a specific ratio, whereas the loss is shared according to the ratio of the contribution made. *Musharaka* is based on a mutual contract and, therefore, it needs to have the following features to enable it to be valid under the *Sharia'a*:

- Parties should be capable of entering into a contract (that is, they should be of legal age).
- The contract must take place with the free consent of the parties (that is, without any duress).

In *Musharaka*, every partner has a right to take part in the management, and to work for it. The partners may agree, however, on a condition in which the management is carried out by one of them, and no other partner works for the *Musharaka*. In such a case the 'sleeping' (silent) partner is entitled to the profit only to the extent of his investment, and the ratio of profit allocated to him should not exceed the relative size of his investment in the business.

If all the partners agree to work for the joint venture, however, each one of them should be treated as the agent of the other in all matters of business. Work done by any of them, in the normal course of business, shall be deemed as being authorised by all partners.

Musharaka can take the form of an unlimited, unrestricted and equal partnership in which the partners enjoy complete equality in the areas of capital, management and right of disposition. Each partner is both the agent and guarantor of the other.

Another more limited investment partnership is also available. This type of partnership occurs when two or more parties contribute to a capital fund, with money, contributions in kind or labour. In this case, each partner is only the agent and not the guarantor of his partner.

For both forms, the partners share profits in an agreed upon manner and bear losses in proportion to the size of their capital contributions.

In conventional banking, 'interest' predetermines a fixed rate of return on a loan advanced by the financier irrespective of the profit earned or loss suffered by the debtor, whereas *Musharaka* does not envisage a fixed rate of return. Instead, the return in *Musharaka* is based on the actual profit earned by the joint venture. The presence of risk in *Musharaka* makes it acceptable as an Islamic financing instrument.

The finance provider of an interest-bearing loan has many techniques open to prevent him suffering a loss in the event of failure of the project, whereas the financier in *Musharaka*, not having these techniques available, can suffer loss if the joint venture fails to produce fruit.

2.4 *SHARIA'A* RULES FOR PROFIT AND LOSS WITH *MUSHARAKA*

2.4.1 Distribution of Profits

The distribution of profits in a *Musharaka* arrangement must abide by two rules:

- The proportion of profit to be distributed between the partners must be agreed upon at the time of effecting the contract. If no such proportion has been determined, the contract is not valid under the *Sharia'a*.
- The ratio of profit for each partner must be determined in proportion to the actual profit accrued to the business, and not in proportion to the capital invested by them. It is not permissible to fix a lump sum amount for any one of the partners, or any rate of profit tied up with their investment.

The effect of these rules is that if 'A' and 'B' enter into a partnership and it is agreed between them that 'A' will be given 10,000 per month as his share in the profit, and the rest will go to 'B', the partnership is deemed to be invalid. Similarly, if it is agreed between them that 'A' will get 15% of his investment, the contract is also invalid. The correct basis for distribution would be an agreed percentage of the actual profit accruing to the business.

If a lump sum amount or a certain percentage of the investment has been agreed for any one of the partners, it must be expressly mentioned, in the agreement, that it will be subject to the final settlement at the end of the term. This means that any amount so drawn by any partner will be treated as 'on account payment' and will be adjusted to the actual profit he may deserve at the end of the term. But if no profit is actually earned, or is less than anticipated, the amount drawn by the partner must be returned.

Under a *Musharaka* contract the profit ratio agreed is not necessarily symmetric to the capital contribution made to the project.

2.4.2 Sharing of Losses

The potential asymmetry of profit distribution, however, does not occur in the event of a loss. Each partner will suffer any loss exactly according to the ratio of his investment. So if a partner has invested 40% of the capital, he must suffer 40% of the loss – no more, no less – and any condition to the contrary renders the contract invalid under the *Sharia'a*.

There is a famous Islamic *Hadith* stating this policy:

> "Profit is based on the agreement of the parties but loss is always subject to the ratio of investment."

Therefore, losses in *Musharaka* are symmetric to the ratio of the capital contribution made.

2.5 MANAGEMENT OF *MUSHARAKA*

The normal principle of *Musharaka* is that every partner has a right to take part in its management and to work for it. The partners can agree, however, upon a condition in which the management will be carried out by one of them, and no other partner will work for the *Musharaka*. In this latter case the sleeping partner is entitled to the profit only to the extent of his investment, and the ratio of profit allocated to him should not exceed the ratio of his investment, as discussed earlier.

However, if all the partners agree to work for the joint venture, each one of them must, under the *Sharia'a*, be treated as the agent of the other in all the matters of the business; any work done by one of them in the normal course of business shall be deemed to be authorised by all the partners.

2.6 *SHARIA'A* RULES FOR *MUSHARAKA*

To be *Sharia'a* compliant, a *Musharaka* must meet the following conditions:

- The capital provided by each partner must be specific, existent and easily accessible. It is inappropriate to establish a company with borrowed money, for the purpose of profit.
- It is permissible for partners to have unequal ownership in the project. The percentage of ownership is set forth in the agreement.

- The capital of the company must be money (liquid cash). Some Jurists permit contributing merchandise as invested capital, but any merchandise must be valued and the value agreed upon by all parties. Once the value has been established it is counted as capital and stipulated in the contract as such.
- It is impermissible to impose conditions forbidding one of the partners from working on the project. The company is built on honour and each partner implicitly permits and gives power of attorney to the other partner(s) to dispose of and work with capital as is deemed necessary to conduct business. However, it is permissible for one partner to have full responsibility for the operations of the company, provided he is granted this authority by the other partners.
- A partner is a trustee of company funds in his possession and is held responsible for their proper use. It is permissible to take a mortgage or a guarantee against company assets, but it is impermissible to take security for profit or capital.
- Each customer/partners' share of the profits must be known in order to avoid uncertainty (*gharar*). Also, it is required that the ownership proportion be in percentage terms and not as a fixed sum, because this would violate the requirements of a partnership.
- In principle, profit must be divided among partners in ratios proportionate to their shares in capital. Some Jurists permit variation in profit shares as long as it is agreed to by all the partners. This may be the case when one of the partners has more business skills and does not agree to parity, so some variation in the sharing of profits becomes necessary.
- In principle, a partnership is a permissible and nonbinding contract. Thus, if a partner wishes, he could rescind the agreement provided that this occurs with the knowledge of the other partner or partners. Rescinding the agreement without the knowledge of the other partners prejudices the rescinding partner's interest. On the other hand some Jurists take the view that the partnership contract is binding up to the liquidation of capital or to the accomplishment of the job specification agreed to on acceptance of the contract.

2.7   CASE 1

Details of four *Musharaka* projects are given in Table 2.1. These projects took place in the Sudan.

Table 2.1   Four Sudanese *Musharaka* projects (£ Sudanese)

Description	Project 1	Project 2	Project 3	Project 4
Projects	*Mobile phone shop*	*Flower nursery*	*Coffee shop*	*Internet cafe*
Capital investment	29,295	200,000	1,000,000	1,000,000
Duration of *Musharaka*	One week	One week	Four months	One month
Bank contribution	75%	50%	50%	14%
Partners contribution	25%	50%	50%	86%
Bank's share in management	0%	0%	1.20%	5%
Partner's share in management	30%	60%	87.70%	25%
Bank's share in total profit	52.50%	20%	6.75%	14.80%
Partner's share in total profit	47.50%	80%	93.25%	85.20%

2.7.1 Questions

1. Calculate the monthly rates of return for each project for the bank and the partner.

_____
_____
_____
_____

2. Calculate the annual rates of return for each project for both parties.

_____
_____
_____
_____

2.8 CASE 2

A Sudanese Islamic bank invested into a grocery store for a one month period, applying a *Musharaka* contract. The investment contributions of the bank and the grocery store partner with the net profit are given in Table 2.2.

Table 2.2 Sudanese bank investment contributions (£ Sudanese)

	Bank	Partner	Total
Investment	735	690	1425
Percentage	52	48	100
Net profit	179	271	450

It was agreed that the profit distribution for the management of the project should be 37% for the bank and 63% for the grocery store manager. The 37% was to be distributed as being 30% of the partner's percentage in the management with the bank contributing 7% of the management.

It was also agreed that the 63% should be divided as being 30% of the partner's percentage of the profit and 33% as being the bank's percentage of the profit.

2.8.1 Questions

Calculate the following:

3. The total amount received by each party (bank and grocery store) as the management share.

_____
_____
_____
_____

4. The total amount received by each party as the shared profit.

5. The grocery store's monthly rate of return.

6. The grocery store's annual rate of return.

7. The bank's monthly rate of return.

8. The bank's annual rate of return.

Case Study 3: Diminishing *Musharaka* Contract

3.1 LEARNING OUTCOMES

After reading Case Study 3 you should be able to do the following:

- Define the Diminishing *Musharaka* contract.
- Distinguish a conventional loan from a Diminishing *Musharaka* contract.
- Describe the elements of a Diminishing *Musharaka* transaction.
- Contrast Diminishing *Musharaka* with the other modes of Islamic finance.
- Identify the Arabic terminology used in Diminishing *Musharaka*.
- Describe the different types of *Musharaka*.
- Identify the reasoning behind the *Sharia'a* rulings on Diminishing *Musharaka*.
- Explain the practicalities of implementing Diminishing *Musharaka*.
- Describe the *Sharia'a* rulings on Diminishing *Musharaka*.
- Identify problems with applying Diminishing *Musharaka*.
- Explain the importance of deferred sales within Islamic finance.
- Contrast the role of penalty defaults within conventional and Islamic finance.
- Explain how Diminishing *Musharaka* can be used for home finance.
- Define LIBOR and explain its application with a Diminishing *Musharaka* contract.

3.2 DIMINISHING *MUSHARAKA* AS A MODE OF ISLAMIC FINANCE

Case Abstract

Islamic financial principles stress the importance of profit and loss share agreements given the impermissibility of using conventional applications of interest in financial transactions. One of the most Islamically acceptable techniques is that of Diminishing *Musharaka*. According to this concept the Islamic bank and its partner/customer participate in the joint ownership of a business/property. The share of the bank is further divided into a number of units and it is understood that the partner/customer will purchase the units of the share of the bank one by one periodically, thus increasing their own share until all the units of the bank are purchased by them. This then makes the partner/customer the sole owner of the business/property. This case study describes the working of the Diminishing *Musharaka* mode of Islamic finance.

3.3 SUMMARY OF DIMINISHING *MUSHARAKA*

Diminishing (or Digressive, as it is sometimes known) *Musharaka* is a special form of *Musharaka*, which ultimately culminates in the ownership of the asset, or the project, by the client. It operates in the following manner.

The Islamic bank participates as a financial partner, in full or in part, in a project with a given income forecast. The partner and the bank sign an agreement that stipulates each party's share of the profits. The agreement, however, also provides payment for a portion of the net income of the project as repayment of the principal financed by the bank. The partner is entitled to keep the rest. In this way, the bank's share of the equity is progressively reduced and the partner eventually becomes the full owner.

When the bank enters into a Diminishing *Musharaka*, its intention is not to stay in the partnership until the company is dissolved. In this type of partnership, the bank agrees to accept payment on an instalment basis or in one lump sum of an amount necessary to buy out the bank's partnership interest. In this way, as the bank receives payments over and above its share in partnership profits. Its partnership interest diminishes until it is completely bought out of the partnership.

After the discharge, the bank withdraws its claims from the deal and the property/business becomes the property of the partner. The decreasing partnership arrangement is an Islamic bank innovation. It differs from the permanent *Musharaka* partnership (see Case Study 2) only in continuity. The intent of the project is capital growth. The project may be profitable or may lose money. In the event of loss each partner bears his share in the loss in the exact proportionate share of capital. If the project is successful, profits are distributed between the two partners (the bank and the customer) in accordance with the agreement.

There are four steps in a Diminishing *Musharaka*:

1. The bank tenders part of the capital required for the project in its capacity as a participant and agrees with the customer/partner on a specific process of gradually selling its share of the capital to the partner.
2. The customer/partner tenders part of the capital required for the project and agrees to pay an agreed-upon amount in return for the ultimate full ownership of the business/property.
3. The bank progressively sells its share of capital. It expresses its readiness, in accordance with the agreement, to sell a specific percentage of its share of capital.
4. The customer/partner pays the price of that percentage of capital to the bank and the ownership is transferred to the customer/partner.

3.4 *SHARIA'A* RULES FOR A DIMINISHING *MUSHARAKA* CONTRACT

In addition to all the *Sharia'a* legal rules that apply to the permanent partnership, which also apply to the diminishing partnership, the following additional *Sharia'a* rules must also be observed:

- The diminishing partnership must not be a mere loan financing operation. In other words, there must be shared ownership and all the parties must share in the profits or losses during the period of the partnership.

- The bank must completely own its share in the partnership and all rights of ownership with regard to management of the business. In the event that the bank authorises its partner to manage the business, the bank has the right of oversight supervision and follow up.
- It is impermissible to include, in the contract of diminishing partnership, a condition that adjudges the customer/partner to return to the bank the total of its shares in capital in addition to profits accruing from that share, because this resembles *riba* (interest).
- It is permissible for the bank to promise to sell its shares in the company to the customer/partner as long as the partner pays the value of the shares. The sale must be concluded as a separate deal from the original contract to purchase the property.

3.5 WHAT IS THE DIFFERENCE BETWEEN *IJARA WA IQTINA* AND DIMINISHING *MUSHARAKA*?

In contrast to the leasing model *Ijara Wa Iqtina*, in which ownership of the financed item remains with the lessor for the entire lease period, ownership in a diminishing partnership is explicitly shared between the customer and the Islamic financial institution. Legally, what is established is an Islamic *Sharikat Al-Milk*. The periodic payments of the customer in this model contain two parts:

- a rental payment for the part of the property owned by the Islamic financial institution; and
- a buy-out of part of that ownership.

Over time, the portion of the asset owned by the customer increases until the customer owns the entire asset and needs to pay no more rent. At that time, the contract is terminated.

3.6 APPLICATIONS OF DIMINISHING *MUSHARAKA*

According to the concept of Diminishing *Musharaka*, a financier and his client participate either in the joint ownership of a property or equipment, or in a joint commercial enterprise. The financier's share is further divided into a number of units and it is understood that the client will purchase these units one by one periodically, thus increasing his own share until all the units of the financier are purchased, so making the client the sole owner of the property, or commercial enterprise, as the case may be.

The Diminishing *Musharaka* concept has taken different shapes in different transactions. Two examples are given in the following sections.

3.6.1 House Purchase

Diminishing *Musharaka* has been mostly used in house financing. The client wants to purchase a house for which he does not have adequate funds. He approaches the financier who agrees to participate with him in purchasing the required house. To take an example, assume 20% of the price is paid by the client and 80% of the price by the financier. Thus the financier owns 80% of the house while the client owns 20%. After purchasing the property jointly, the client uses the house for his residential requirements and pays rent to the financier for using his share in the property. At the same time the share of the financier is further divided into eight equal units, each unit representing 10% ownership of the house.

The client promises the financier that he will purchase say one unit every three months. Accordingly, after the first term of three months he purchases one unit of the share of the financier by paying one-tenth of the house price. This reduces the share of the financier from 80% to 70%. Hence, the rent payable to the financier is also reduced to that extent. At the end of the second term, the client purchases another unit thereby increasing his share in the property to 40% and reducing the share of the financier to 60% and consequentially reducing the rent to that proportion. This process goes on in the same fashion until, after the end of two years, the client purchases the whole share of the financier thereby reducing the share of the financier to zero and increasing his own share to 100%.

This arrangement allows the financier to claim rent according to his proportion of ownership in the property and, at the same time, allows him periodical return of a part of his principal through purchases of the units of his share of the property.

3.6.2   Service Sector

Assume that 'A' wants to purchase a taxi and use it for offering transport services to passengers and earning income through fares recovered from them, but 'A' is short of funds. 'B' agrees to participate in the purchase of the taxi. Therefore, both purchase a taxi jointly. 'B' pays 80% of the price and 'A' pays 20%.

After the taxi is purchased, it is employed to provide taxi rides whereby the net income of say £1000 is earned on a daily basis. Since 'B' has an 80% share in the taxi, it is agreed that 80% of the fare will be given to him and 20% will be retained by 'A', who has a 20% share in the taxi. Therefore, on a daily basis 'B' earns £800 and 'A' earns £200. At the same time the share of 'B' is further divided into eight units.

Every three months 'A' purchases one unit from the share of 'B'. Consequently the share of 'B' is reduced to 70% and the share of 'A' is increased to 30%, meaning thereby that, as from that date, 'A' will be entitled to £300 from the daily income of the taxi and 'B' will earn £700. This process continues until after the expiry of two years 'A' owns the whole taxi and 'B' will have been repaid his original investment along with the income distributed to him.

3.7   CASE ASSUMPTIONS

When used in home financing, *Musharaka* is frequently applied as a diminishing partnership. In home financing the customer forms a partnership with an Islamic financial institution for the purchase of a property. The financial institution rents out its part of the property to the client and receives compensation in the form of the rent received, which is based on a mutually agreed fair market value. Any amount paid above the rental value increases the share of the customer in the property and reduces the share of the financial institution.

3.8   *SHARIA'A* CONSIDERATIONS TO BE NOTED

The agreement of joint purchase, leasing and selling different units of the share of the bank should not be tied up together in one single contract.

At the time of the purchase of each unit, the sale must be effected by the exchange of offer and acceptance at that particular date.

3.9 PRACTICAL SHAPE OF THE TRANSACTION

The customer and the bank buy a house for £10 million, the bank contributing 80% of the price, by paying £8 million, and the customer contributing 20% of the price, by paying £2 million;

The price of the house is further sub-divided into 10 units where the bank owns 8 units and the customer owns 2 units:

Say that the total rent of the house is £75,000 per month, in which case the rent of one unit is £7500 per month.

The bank gives its 8 units on *Ijara* (lease) to the customer for £60,000 per month.

3.10 CASE STUDY QUESTIONS

1. Based on the rental value and the financing period, determine the monthly repayment schedule that results in the client fully owning the property at the end of the agreed rental term.

   _____

   _____

   _____

   _____

2. Detail any assumptions you have made to undertake these calculations.

   _____

   _____

   _____

   _____

4

Case Study 4: *Mudaraba* Contract

4.1 LEARNING OUTCOMES

After working through Case Study 4 you should be able to do the following:

- Define the *Mudaraba* contract.
- Explain the treatment of money within Islam.
- Distinguish a conventional loan from a *Mudaraba* contract.
- Describe the elements of a *Mudaraba* transaction.
- Contrast *Mudaraba* with the other modes of Islamic finance.
- Describe the different types of *Mudaraba*.
- Identify the Arabic terminology used in *Mudaraba*.
- Explain the practicalities of implementing *Mudaraba*.
- Identify the reasoning behind the *Sharia'a* rulings on *Mudaraba*.
- Explain the practicalities of implementing two-tier *Mudaraba*.
- Describe the *Sharia'a* rulings on *Mudaraba*.
- Identify problems with applying *Mudaraba*.
- Explain the importance of deferred sales within Islamic finance.
- Explain how *Mudaraba* can be used for home finance.
- Identify the deferred sale versus profit and loss share contracts.
- Explain how *Mudaraba* can be used for Islamic fund management.

4.2 *MUDARABA* AS A MODE OF ISLAMIC FINANCE

Case Abstract

Within the Islamic financial system the purest alternative to charging and receiving interest is financing on a profit and loss partnership basis. The basic principle of profit and loss sharing (PLS) is that, instead of lending money at a fixed rate of return, the banker forms a partnership with the borrower thereby sharing in a venture's profits and losses. *Mudaraba* is a form of partnership where one party provides the funds while the other provides the expertise and management. Any profits are shared between the two parties according to pre-agreed ratios, whereas any loss is borne only by the provider of the capital. This case study describes the workings of the *Mudaraba* contract.

4.3 *MUDARABA* AND PLS – PURE ISLAMIC BANKING

The basic principle of PLS is that, instead of lending money at a fixed rate of return, the banker forms a partnership with the borrower thereby sharing in a venture's profits and losses. If the returns are good the profits are shared equitably, and so the return to the investors depends on the profitability of the investment. Nothing is pre-fixed.

The PLS system allows a capital-poor, but potentially promising, entrepreneur to obtain financing. The bank, being an investor, has a stake in the success of the venture.

The principle applied is that the entrepreneur, rather than being concerned with debt-servicing, can concentrate on a long-term endeavour that in turn will hopefully bring economic and social benefits to the community, as well as to the parties concerned. Muslims argue that this system is fairer to both parties in the transaction, with the effect that no one exploits anyone else.

The two 'purest' forms of PLS are *Mudaraba*, which comes in Tier 1 and Tier 2 versions, and *Musharaka*.

Mudaraba is a form of partnership in which one party provides the funds while the other provides the expertise and management. The two parties share any profits between them according to pre-agreed ratios, but any loss is borne by the provider of the capital alone.

In contrast, *Musharaka* is a partnership agreement whereby an Islamic bank provides funds, which are mixed with the funds of the business enterprise, and sometimes others. All the providers of capital are entitled to participate in management but are not necessarily required to do so. Under the *Sharia'a* the profit must be distributed among the partners in pre-agreed ratios, and any loss is borne strictly in proportion to respective capital contributions.

4.3.1   *Mudaraba* – Profit Sharing Agreement

The *Mudaraba* contract is structured between the supplier of capital and the entrepreneur who services it. One party supplies the capital to a second entrepreneurial party (the *Mudarib*) for the processing of some business activity on the condition that the resulting profits are distributed in mutually agreed proportions and all capital loss is borne by the provider of the capital. In the latter case, the entrepreneur does bear some loss – the opportunity cost of his time and labour – but not any direct financial loss.

The *Mudaraba* contract is a contract between two parties whereby one party, the *Rab ul Mall* (the sleeping partner or beneficiary), entrusts money to the other party, the *Mudarib* (the working partner or managing trustee). The *Mudarib* agrees to use the money in an agreed manner and then return to the *Rab ul Mall* the principal and the pre-agreed share of the profit. The *Mudarib* is then rewarded with the pre-agreed share of the profit.

The predominant manifestation of *Mudaraba* is the two-tier *Mudaraba* model. The first tier (liability side) is formed when depositors place their funds with an Islamic financial institution that takes up the role of the *Mudarib*. *Mudaraba* here is the investment deposits side of the Islamic bank's balance sheet. The bank then invests these deposits with entrepreneurs in the second tier (asset side) where the bank acts as the capital investor. Islamic financial institutions' profits arise from a percentage of the returns from the second-tier *Mudaraba*.

The following *Sharia'a* characteristics of *Mudaraba* are of significance:

- The division of profits between the two parties must necessarily be on a proportional basis and cannot be a lump-sum or guaranteed return.
- The investor is not liable for losses beyond the capital he has contributed.
- The *Mudarib* does not share in the monetary losses except for the loss of his own time and effort.
- The *Mudaraba* can be general purpose (unrestricted *Mudaraba*) or for a specific purpose (restricted *Mudaraba*).

As regards this last point, when the financial institution invests its own capital, alongside the capital procured by the bank with the depositors' funds, this is known as a profit sharing unrestricted investment account.

The unrestricted mode of *Mudaraba* is identical to an investment fund in which managers handle a pool of funds. The agent-manager has relatively limited liability while having sufficient incentives to perform. The capital is invested in broadly defined activities and the terms of profit and risk sharing are customised for such investment. The maturity structures range from short to medium term and it is suitable for commercial activities.

Mudaraba offers the opportunity of pure finance in the sense that the owner of the capital can invest without having to manage personally the capital investment and without having to be exposed to unlimited liabilities. However, *Mudaraba* (and *Musharaka*) are distinct from conventional lending with interest receivables in that, it is argued, they maintain a fair balance between the owner of the capital and the entrepreneur who implements it. Distribution of profits is agreed according to a predetermined proportion of the total and each party only loses what they put into the investment, be it capital or labour. As *Sharia'a* scholars put it:

> "It is important to note that in *Mudaraba* and *Musharaka* the principal amount of funds and a fixed profit cannot be guaranteed."

Box 4.1 illustrates the *Mudaraba* terminology.

Box 4.1 *Mudaraba* terminology

Mudaraba – Tier 1
Rab ul Mall: Bank depositor as supplier/owner of capital; contributes capital, no expertise
Mudarib: Islamic bank as demander of capital; contributes expertise, no capital
Mudaraba – Tier 2
Rab ul Mall: Islamic bank as supplier/owner of capital; contributes capital, no expertise
Mudarib: Borrower-entrepreneur as demander as of capital; contributes expertise, no capital

---

4.3.2 *Sharia'a* Rules for *Mudaraba*

With a two-tier *Mudaraba*, the bank and the *Mudarib*, as depositor, pool funds to fund a specific enterprise. In this case they are both fund providers (*Rab ul Mall*). The *Mudarib* fee could be a fixed fee (to cover management expenses) and a percentage of the profits, or a combination of the two.

A pure form of *Mudaraba* is based on PLS, and in this case the only reward to the *Mudarib* is the profit share. The balance of the profit of the enterprise, after deducting the profit share due to the *Mudarib*, is payable to the bank.

If the enterprise makes a loss the capital providers make the losses.

If the *Mudarib* receives a fee, and any losses are due to negligence on his part, then he forgoes the fee.

4.3.2.1   *The* **Mudaraba Sharia'a** *PLS Allocation Rules*

No co-mingling of funds

In this case, the bank and the *Mudarib* (entrepreneur) do not accrue profit share of the same amount. The *Mudarib* can provide capital as well as management expertise and labour. The bank only provides capital.

Where there is no capital sharing but only profit and loss sharing, the PLS *Mudaraba* split will be directly as agreed – say 50/50.

Co-mingling of funds

When there is co-mingling of funds between the *Mudarib* and the bank (*Mudaraba* funds), the *Mudarib* becomes a partner in respect of his funds and a *Mudarib* in respect of the capital provider. The profit earned on the co-mingled funds will be divided proportionately to the amounts contributed. The effect is that the *Mudarib* takes the profit attributable to his own funds, both capital share and profits share. The remaining profit is distributed between the *Mudarib* and the capital provider according to the provisions of the *Mudaraba* contract.

There is no co-mingling of funds permitted under the standard *Mudaraba* contract.

4.4   CASE 1: *SHARIA'A* ISLAMIC BANK

The relationship between the *Sharia'a* Islamic Bank and its investment account holders is governed by the *Mudaraba* contract, as shown in Table 4.1.

Table 4.1   *Sharia'a* Islamic Bank: *Mudaraba* accounts

Average funds available for investment	Dinars	Dinars	Investment rate
Shareholders	–	130,000,000	100%
Investment Accounts: One Year	150,000,000	–	90%
Investment Accounts: Six Months	450,000,000	–	80%
Investment Savings Accounts*	700,000,000	1300,000,000	60%
Total funds available for investment		1430,000,000	
Profit-sharing ratio:		Mudarib	Depositors
Investment Accounts: One Year		15%	85%
Investment Accounts: Six Months		20%	80%
Investment Savings Accounts		30%	70%
Income for allocation			
Income to be allocated	75,000,000		

* These are investment accounts for short periods

4.4.1   Case 1 Questions

1. Calculate the profit allocated to shareholders and to each class of profit-sharing accounts before and after the *Mudarib* share has been paid.

2. Calculate the rate of return for shareholders and each class of investment account after the *Mudarib* share has been paid.

_____

_____

_____

_____

Please fill in Table 4.2 as part of your answer.

Table 4.2   Profit and rate of return calculation

	(1) Average funds available for investments	(2) Investment rate	(3) Weighted average of invested funds (1 × 2)	(4) Percentage of weighted average of invested funds
Shareholders				
Investment accounts: one year				
Investment accounts: six months				
Investment savings accounts				
Total funds available for investment				

	(5) Net profit from investments (millions)	(6) Shareholders' share of net profit before the *Mudarib* share (4 × 5)	(7) Shareholders' share of the *Mudarib*'s profit*	(8) Distributable profit after shareholders' share of the *Mudarib*'s profit (6 − 7)**	(9) Rate of return (8/1)
Shareholders					
Investment accounts: one year					
Investment accounts: six months					
Investment savings accounts					
Total funds available for investment					

* Column six multiplied by shareholders' ratio of profit allocation.
** Residual accruing to shareholders after payment to investment account holders.

4.5 *MUDARABA* CONTRACT WITH VARIOUS PARTNERS

This section illustrates how a simple *Mudaraba* contract can be made more flexible.

Often a contract may be combined with various other mechanisms for fund raising. In such a facility, a variety of *Mudarib*/entrepreneur relationships can contribute to the capital of the venture as does the *Rab ul Mall* financier.

For each of the five *Mudaraba* cases listed below, both profitable and unprofitable scenarios are possible. For each case study, you are asked to calculate the following and make clear any assumptions that you have made:

- In the case of profits, the actual profits and capital share received by all the parties.
- In the case of losses, the amount of capital that is returned to all the parties.

4.5.1 Case 2 Questions

The *Mudarib* contributes none of his own capital into the project. The bank contributes capital of 100 on a *Mudaraba* basis. No other capital sources are used. PLS is agreed at a ratio of 50/50. Profits are paid to the *Mudarib* as a reward for the successful operation of the business. The balance of any profit is paid to the other partner(s) in the scheme.

Provide the solutions to two potential outcomes:

3. Profits of 10 are made
4. Losses of 10 are made

3._____

_____

_____

_____

4._____

_____

_____

_____

4.5.2 Case 3 Questions

The *Mudarib* contributes 100 of his own capital into the project. The bank contributes capital of 100 on a *Mudaraba* basis. No other capital sources are used. PLS is agreed at a ratio of 50/50. Profits are paid to the *Mudarib* as a reward for the successful operation of the business. The balance of any profit is paid to the other partner(s) in the scheme.

Provide the solutions to two potential outcomes:

5. Profits of 20 are made
6. Losses of 20 are made

✐ 5._____

_____

_____

_____

✐ 6._____

_____

_____

_____

4.5.3   Case 4 Questions

The *Mudarib* borrows 100 capital from the bank which he invests into the project. This loan must be repaid at the maturity of the project whether profits or losses are made. The bank contributes capital of 100. No other capital sources are used. PLS is agreed at a ratio of 50/50. Profits are paid to the *Mudarib* as a reward for the successful operation of the business. The balance of any profit is paid to the other partner(s) in the scheme.

Provide the solutions to two potential outcomes:

7. Profits of 20 are made

8. Losses of 20 are made

✐ 7._____

_____

_____

_____

✐ 8._____

_____

_____

_____

4.5.4   Case 5 Questions

The *Mudarib* acquires 100 capital through a third party *Mudaraba*. The *Mudarib* invests 100 of his own capital into the project. The bank contributes capital of 100. No other capital sources are used. PLS is agreed at a ratio of 33/33/33. Profits are paid to the *Mudarib* as a reward for the successful operation of the business. The balance of any profit is paid to the other partner(s) in the scheme.

Provide the solutions to two potential outcomes:

9. Profits of 30 are made

10. Losses of 30 are made

✎ 9._____

_____

_____

_____

✎ 10._____

_____

_____

_____

4.5.5 Case 6 Questions

The *Mudarib* acquires 100 capital from a business partner. The *Mudarib* invests none of his own capital into the project. The bank agrees to the partnership agreement and contributes capital of 100. No other capital sources are used. The *Mudarib* and the partner agree a PLS ratio of 50/50. The bank and the *Mudarib* agree that the bank will receive half of the profit earned by the *Mudarib*. Profits are paid to the *Mudarib* as a reward for the successful operation of the business. The balance of any profit is paid to the other partner(s) in the scheme.

Provide the solutions to two potential outcomes:

11. Profits of 20 are made
12. Losses of 20 are made

✎ 11._____

_____

_____

_____

✎ 12._____

_____

_____

_____

5

Case Study 5: *Murabaha, Musharaka, Ijara* and *Ijara wa Iqtina* Contracts

5.1 LEARNING OUTCOMES

After working through Case Study 5, you should be able to do the following:

- Distinguish between the alternative Islamic modes of finance.
- Explain how an *Ijara* contract can be applied.
- Describe the *Musharaka* contract rules regarding profits and losses.
- Contrast the *Ijara* with the *Ijara wa Iqtina Sharia'a* rulings.
- Explain how *Mudaraba* can be used with car financing.
- Explain how *Murabaha* can be used with car financing.

5.2 CASE 1: *MURABAHA* CONTRACT

By looking at the issues from the perspectives of an Islamic bank and a conventional bank, demonstrate in what sense *Murabaha* differs from conventional bank lending.

Answer the following questions for both a conventional bank loan and *Murabaha*.

1. What are the key areas of concern?

    ✏ Conventional bank loan _____

    _____

    Murabaha _____

    _____

2. How would you categorise the bank–customer relationship?

    ✏ Conventional bank loan _____

    _____

    Murabaha _____

    _____

3. Are the returns fixed or variable?

    ✏ Conventional bank loan _____

    _____

    Murabaha _____

4. Are there any guarantees

   ✐Conventional bank loan _____

   _____

   Murabaha _____

   _____

5. What happens if the borrower defaults?

   ✐Conventional bank loan _____

   _____

   Murabaha _____

   _____

5.3   CASE 2: *MUSHARAKA* CONTRACT

5.3.1   *Musharaka* with Profits

Assume the following:

- A company is importing and selling Mercedes cars.
- An Islamic bank invests US$8 million for an 80% profit share.
- An investor invests US$2 million for a 20% profit share.
- The investor is to be paid a 10% management fee as percentage of profit after expenses.

Assume:

$$\text{Sale proceeds} = \text{US\$12,400,000}$$
$$\text{Expenses} = \text{US\$200,000}$$

Calculate:

6. The total return to the bank:

   ✐_____

   _____

   _____

   _____

7. The total return to the investor:

   ✐_____

   _____

   _____

   _____

5.3.2   *Musharaka* with Losses

Same assumptions as in Section 5.3.1 but now assume:

$$\text{Sale proceeds} = \text{US\$9,200,000}$$
$$\text{Expenses} = \text{US\$200,000}$$

Calculate:

8. The total return to the bank:

_____

_____

_____

_____

9. The total return to the investor:

_____

_____

_____

_____

5.4   CASE 3: *IJARA*: OPERATING LEASE CONTRACT

A bank customer requests financing for five air conditioning units (A/Cs) on a three-year lease from the bank.

The bank buys the assets and leases them for three years.

Financial details		US$
Cost of A/Cs		10,000
Five-year life – annual depreciation		2000 p.a.
Insurance (*Takaful*)		600 p.a.
Profit required by the bank	Year 1	900
	Year 2	700
	Year 3	500

10. What is the yearly *Ijara* rental the bank will charge in order to cover the costs and to make the required profit?

_____

_____

_____

_____

5.5   CASE 4: *IJARA WA IQTINA*: FINANCE LEASE CONTRACT

A bank customer requests financing for five air conditioning units (A/Cs) on a three-year lease from the bank.

A bank buys assets and leases them for three years.

Financial details		US$
Cost of A/Cs		10,000
Profit required by the bank	Year 1	900
	Year 2	700
	Year 3	500

The lessee pays the insurance (*Takaful*)

11. What is the yearly rental the bank will charge in order to cover the costs and to make the required profit?

_____

_____

_____

_____

5.6   CASE 5: *MUDARABA* WITH *MURABAHA* CONTRACTS

5.6.1   Car *Mudaraba* with *Murabaha*

Assume the following:

- An Islamic bank provides the capital to the *Mudaraba*.
- The *Mudarib* buys cars from the dealer on a spot basis.
- The *Mudarib* sells the cars to the buyer on deferred payment basis at cost plus a mark-up on a 36-month-instalment basis (*Murabaha* sale).
- The buyer will start repayment at the end of the first month.
- Each month the *Mudarib* will deposit the monthly repayment with the bank.

12. Design a flow chart to demonstrate the role played by each party in this transaction, defining all the terms used.

6

Case Study 6: Islamic Home Finance

6.1 LEARNING OUTCOMES

After working through Case Study 6 you should be able to do the following:

- Explain how a *Sharia'a*-compliant mortgage works.
- Distinguish a conventional mortgage from a *Sharia'a*-compliant mortgage.
- Describe how a *Murabaha* mortgage works.
- Describe how an *Ijara wa Iqtina* mortgage works.
- Describe how a Diminishing *Musharaka* mortgage works.
- Describe how an *Istisna'a* mortgage works.
- Identify the principles underlying the Manzil *Murabaha* Home Purchase mortgage.
- Explain the principles underlying the Devon Bank Residential *Murabaha* Home Purchase mortgage.
- Identify the principles underlying the Manzil *Ijara* Home Purchase mortgage.
- Explain the principles underlying the Devon Bank Residential *Ijara* Home Purchase mortgage.

6.2 *SHARIA'A*-COMPLIANT MORTGAGES

Case Abstract

Islamic financial principles stress the importance of profit and loss share agreements given the impermissibility of using conventional applications of 'interest' in financial transactions. A conventional interest paying mortgage would not be *Sharia'a* compliant. With regards to house purchase, four Islamically acceptable techniques are available: *Murabaha*, *Ijara wa Iqtina*, Diminishing *Musharaka* and *Istisna'a*. This case study describes the applications of *Sharia'a*-compliant home financing techniques.

6.3 *SHARIA'A*-COMPLIANT STRUCTURES FOR ISLAMIC HOME FINANCE

Four structures have been used to assist Muslims to acquire their homes in a manner consistent with the *Sharia'a*:

- *Murabaha*;
- *Ijara wa Iqtina*;
- Diminishing *Musharaka*;
- *Istisna'a*.

6.3.1 *Murabaha*

Literally, *Murabaha* means a profitable sale and it is also sometimes called *Bai' Bithaman Ajil*, meaning deferred payment sale. *Murabaha*, in this context, is essentially an instalment sales contract for property. Of all the Islamic approaches to the question of leveraged home acquisition or investor funded home acquisition, this method is most consistent with the conventional house purchase processes.

Murabaha is a form of asset finance that involves the lender purchasing the asset, back to back with a sale of the asset, to the borrower, at an increased price. This increased price reflects the interest otherwise payable.

Details of the Manzil and Devon Bank *Murabaha* schemes are given in Appendices 1 and 2 at the end of this Case.

6.3.2 *Ijara wa Iqtina*

In this transaction, the customer (lessee) selects a property and the investor buys it. The investor (lessor) then agrees an operating property lease with the customer/bank. The investor promises to sell and the customer promises to buy the property. The customer pays rent, as well as contributing to a savings fund, which is structured to accrete to a level allowing the customer to buy out the property from the investor. The savings fund may be initiated with a large initial payment similar to a conventional down-payment.

In this process, the investor profits from the customer's rental payments for use of the property and the customer makes monthly payments, on account, to buy out the investor's estate according to a pre-agreed schedule.

In an *Ijara wa Iqtina* contract, a lease is written, with an additional promise by the lessor that he will agree to sell the leased object at the end of the lease at a predetermined residual value. This promise is binding on the lessor only, and the lessee has the option of purchasing the item at the end of the lease, or returning it to the owner-lessor.

The lessor in the *Ijara wa Iqtina* contract is the financier/bank and the lessee is the customer.

A common model for equipment, car and house financing in North America is based on leasing or lease-purchase. Under the Islamic equivalent, the Islamic financial institution buys the financed asset and retains the title through the life of the contract. The customer makes a series of lease payments over a specified period of time, and may have the option at the end to buy the item from the lessor (and owner) at a pre-specified residual value. The period of the lease and the rent payments may be made such that the final payment is only symbolic.

The concept requires a *Sharia'a* modification to the conventional house purchase process to allow the investor or the bank to take the place of the consumer in the purchase contract. One strength of this approach is that *Sharia'a* scholars are comfortable with the securitisation of leased assets and a variety of investors are willing to buy such assets.

A weakness with this concept is that tax deductibility is likely, but not explicit. Another issue, in the United States and elsewhere, is to what degree landlord-tenant issues such as rent control or eviction rights, which may be fixed by state and local laws, may apply to this transaction as a lease distinct from a means to acquire a home.

Details of the Manzil and the Devon Bank *Ijara* schemes are given in Appendices 3 and 4 at the end of this Case.

6.3.3 Diminishing *Musharaka*

Diminishing (or Digressive) *Musharaka* is a special form of *Musharaka*, which ultimately culminates in the ownership of the asset, or the project, by the client. The principles which would be applied for any project, including home finance are discussed below. It operates in the following manner.

The Islamic bank participates as a financial partner, in full or in part, in a project with a given income forecast. An agreement is signed by the partner and the bank, which stipulates each party's share of the profits. However, the agreement also provides payment for a portion of the net income of the project as repayment of the principal financed by the bank. The partner is entitled to keep the rest. In this way, the bank's share of the equity is progressively reduced and the partner eventually becomes the full owner.

When the bank enters into a Diminishing *Musharaka* its intention is not to stay in the partnership until the company is dissolved. In this type of partnership, the bank agrees to accept payment on an instalment basis, or in one lump sum, of an amount necessary to buy the bank's partnership interest. In this way as the bank receives payments, over and above its share in partnership profits, its partnership interest reduces until it is completely bought out of the partnership.

After the discharge, the bank withdraws its claims from the firm and it becomes the property of the partner. The decreasing partnership arrangement is an Islamic bank innovation. It differs from the permanent *Musharaka* partnership only in continuity. The intent of the project is capital growth. The project may be profitable or lose money. In the event of loss each partner bears his share in the loss in his exact proportionate share of capital. In the event that the project is successful, profits are distributed between the two partners (the bank and the customer) in accordance with the agreement.

There are four steps in a Diminishing *Musharaka* as applied to home finance

1. The bank tenders part of the capital required for the house purchase in its capacity as a participant and agrees with the customer/partner on a specific method of gradually selling its share of the house back to the partner.
2. The customer/partner tenders part of the capital required for the house and agrees to pay an agreed upon amount and rent in return for the ultimate full ownership of the property.
3. The bank progressively sells its share of capital. The bank expresses its readiness, in accordance with the agreement, to sell a specific percentage of its share of capital with the rental element decreasing.
4. The customer/partner pays the price of that percentage of capital to the bank and the ownership is transferred to the customer/partner.

6.3.3.1 Sharia'a *Rules for Permanent* Musharaka

The main *Sharia'a* requirements applying to permanent *Musharaka* are as follows:

* It is a condition that the capital provided by each partner is specific, existent and easily accessible. It is inappropriate to establish a company with borrowed money, for the purpose of profit.
* It is permissible for partners to have unequal ownership in the project. The percentage of ownership is set forth in the agreement.
* It is a condition that the capital of the company is money (cash). Some Jurists permit contributing merchandise as invested capital. However, any merchandise must be valued,

and the value agreed upon by all parties. Once the value has been established it is counted as capital and stipulated in the contract as such.

- It is impermissible to impose conditions forbidding one of the partners from working on the project. Each partner implicitly permits and gives power of attorney to the other partner(s) to dispose of and work with capital as is deemed necessary to conduct business. However, it is permissible for one partner to have full responsibility for the operations of the company, provided he is granted this authority by the other partners.
- A partner is a trustee of company funds in his possession and is held responsible for their proper use. It is permissible to take a mortgage or a guarantee against company assets, but it is impermissible to take security for profit or capital.
- It is a condition that each customers'/partners' share of the profits be known in order to avoid uncertainty (*gharar*). Also, it is required that the ownership interest be in percentage terms and not as a fixed sum, because this would violate the requirements of a partnership.
- In principle profit must be divided among partners in ratios proportionate to their shares in capital. Some Jurists permit variation in profit shares as long as it is agreed to by all the partners. This may be the case when one of the partners has more business skills and does not agree to parity, and so some variation in the sharing of profits becomes necessary.
- In principle, a partnership is a permissible and nonbinding contract. Thus, if a partner wishes, he could rescind the agreement provided that this occurs with the knowledge of the other partner or partners. Rescinding the agreement without the knowledge of the other partners' prejudices the rescinding partner's interest. On the other hand some Jurists take the view that the partnership contract is binding up to the liquidation of capital or to the accomplishment of the job specification agreed to on acceptance of the contract.

6.3.3.2   Sharia'a *Rules for Diminishing* Musharaka

In addition to all the *Sharia'a* legal rules that apply to the permanent *Musharaka*, which also apply to the Diminishing *Musharaka*, the following *Sharia'a* rules also must be observed:

- It is a condition in the Diminishing *Musharaka* that it is not a mere loan financing operation. In other words there must be shared ownership and all the parties must share in the profits or losses during the period of the *Musharaka*.
- It is a condition that the bank must completely own its share in the partnership and all rights of ownership with regard to management of the business. In the event that the bank authorises its partner to manage the business, the bank has the right of oversight supervision and follow up.
- It is impermissible to include in the contract of Diminishing *Musharaka* a condition that adjudges the customer/partner to return to the bank the total of its shares in capital in addition to profits accruing from that share, because this resembles *riba* (interest).
- It is permissible for the bank to offer a promise to sell its shares in the company to the customer/partner if the partner pays the value of the shares. The sale must be concluded as a separate deal.

6.3.4   What is the Difference between *Ijara wa Iqtina* and Diminishing *Musharaka*?

In contrast to the *Ijara* leasing model, where ownership of the financed item remains with the lessor for the entire lease period, ownership in a Diminishing *Musharaka* is explicitly shared between the customer and the Islamic financial institution. Legally, what is established is an Islamic *Sharikat Al-Milk*.

The periodic payments of the customer in the Diminishing *Musharaka* model contain two parts:

- A rental payment for the part of the property owned by the Islamic financial institution.
- A buy-out of part of that ownership.

Over time, the portion of the asset owned by the customer increases, until he owns the entire asset and needs to pay no more rent. At that time, the contract is terminated.

6.3.5   Applications of Diminishing *Musharaka*

According to this concept, a financier and his client participate either in the joint ownership of a property or equipment, or in a joint commercial enterprise. The share of the financier is further divided into a number of units and it is understood that the client will purchase the units of the share of the financier one by one periodically, thus increasing his own share until all the units of the financier are purchased by him so as to make him the sole owner of the property, or the commercial enterprise, as the case may be.

Details of the Meezan Bank Diminishing *Musharaka* are given in Appendix 5.

6.3.6   *Istisna'a* Contract

Istisna'a is an Islamic term meaning 'manufacturing' and is applied to construction finance.

With an *Istisna'a* contract the consumer asks the bank to finance the construction of a house. The bank engages a builder or the consumer to build, with the bank's funds, the desired structure or property that the bank has purchased. Upon completion of the development, there may be an outright cash sale, a *Murabaha* sale, an *Ijara wa Iqtina* lease or a Diminishing *Musharaka* partnership.

6.4   APPENDIX 1: MANZIL HOME PURCHASE PLANS (*MURABAHA*)

6.4.1   *Murabaha* ('Deferred Sale Finance')

Murabaha was first introduced in Pakistan in 1997 and is a simple method of financing house purchase according to Islamic principles. Ahli United Bank have created a *Sharia'a*-compliant form of house finance known as the Manzil House Purchase Plan.

6.4.2   How Does the Manzil Home Purchase Plan Work?

The customer identifies the property he wishes to buy and agrees the purchase price with the seller of the property, in the normal way:

1. The customer approaches Manzil for assistance and completes an application form.
2. Manzil will buy the property, after solicitors have confirmed that everything is in order, and immediately sell it to the buyer at a higher price.
3. The higher price is calculated based on the value of the property, the number of years the customer wishes to repay over and the amount of the customer's first down payment.

4. When purchased, the property is registered in the customer's name and the sale between the customer and the bank is recorded in the *Murabaha* contract.
5. The customer's first payment to the bank is made on the day of completion and is the customer's initial contribution, normally a minimum of 17% of the purchase price.
6. One month after completion the customer's regular monthly payments will commence. These will be claimed by direct debit automatically from the customer's normal bank account.

Source: Ahli United Bank

6.5 APPENDIX 2: DEVON BANK

6.5.1 Residential *Murabaha* Purchase Agreement

Devon Bank, a community bank based in Chicago, USA, strives to satisfy the financial services needs of a diverse customer base. This includes providing for religious-based financial transactions such as those required by Islamic religious law (*Sharia'a*).

Islamic law prohibits the paying of interest to a bank in lending transactions (although it allows for the payment of 'profit'), and so Devon Bank strives to accommodate these religious restrictions while still providing the financial assistance a customer may need to purchase a home.

Devon Bank's lending policy is to provide rates competitive with its peers. The bank attempts to translate that policy into practice in its religious finance programmes where the collection of interest is prohibited. However, religious-based financial transactions often do have some additional costs associated with them that may exceed those of non-*Sharia' a*-compliant financing transactions. The amount of additional cost depends on the level of complexity and documentation required to satisfy particular religious concerns.

A *Murabaha* contract provides a suitable mechanism to purchase a home without significant additional complexity, but still allows for a purchase to be structured as an interest-free transaction. A 'standard' *Murabaha* transaction involves a purchase and deferred payment resale.

The customer identifies the home he would like Devon Bank to purchase on his behalf. The customer negotiates the price and other aspects of the purchase. He makes any necessary initial payment to reserve the home and makes sure that the purchase contract allows Devon Bank to step into the transaction as the buyer.

Devon Bank then buys the property. The bank then immediately sells the property to the customer for a fixed price – the purchase price the bank paid plus the bank's profit. This total price is then paid by the customer to the bank in an initial down-payment and in fixed instalments over an agreed-upon period of time.

All direct costs borne by Devon Bank (such as appraisal fees, taxes, recording costs etc.) are paid by the customer at closing. A deposit is made upon the issuance of a commitment, which is applied to such costs at closing. Once the transaction closes, other than a few additional religiously required accommodations such as those dealing with prepayments, the relationship is treated similarly to that as when using a conventional mortgage.

The customer will sign a *Murabaha* purchase agreement with Devon Bank that states that it is an interest-free transaction. The bank is required, however, to calculate a corresponding interest rate, and disclose the rate to the customer in a US government-required manner. Devon

Bank is also required to send disclosures to the customer showing 'interest' paid at the end of each year – which may be tax deductible.

Source: Devon Bank

6.6 APPENDIX 3: MANZIL HOME PURCHASE PLANS (*IJARA*)

6.6.1 *Ijara* ('Lease-to-Own')

Ijara is a popular method of house finance for Muslims. This is because it is more flexible than *Murabaha* in the event that the client wishes to repay early or wants to make additional 'lump sum' payments.

6.6.2 How does it Work?

The customer identifies the property that he wants to buy and agrees the purchase price with the seller in the normal way.

1. The customer approaches Manzil for assistance and completes an application form.
2. Manzil buys the property in its name, after solicitors have confirmed that everything is in order.
3. Manzil then sells the property to the customer as detailed in an agreement titled 'Promise to Purchase'. The purchase price between Manzil and the customer is the same price as the original purchase price.
4. At the same time the customer enters into a lease with Manzil, which details his rights to occupy the property.
5. Once the property is purchased the customer makes monthly payments to Manzil.
6. Each monthly payment is calculated so that part is applied towards the purchase of the property from Manzil and part is applied as rent.
7. The payments are fixed every 12 months, April to April. At the beginning of April each year, Manzil reassesses the rent and payments are likely to vary.
8. The customer may purchase the property from Manzil, at any time, by paying the balance of the purchase price.

Under the Manzil *Ijara* scheme, the property is registered in the bank's name, not just initially, but throughout the period of the lease. The tenant, or lessee, agrees at the outset to purchase the entire property eventually, but at the original price that the bank paid without any mark-up. The monthly payments by the client comprise three elements:

- The repayments of the funds that the bank has used to purchase the property.
- The rent on the property, which is the source of the bank's profit. The rent is reassessed annually to ensure that the bank is making a reasonable return and is adjusted downward to reflect payments already made.
- An insurance rent to recover the cost of the insurance that the bank has to pay on the property.

Over time the monthly payments may increase or reduce or both, depending on the size of the first repayment element that the client decides he can afford. Early repayment could be potentially unprofitable for the bank, unless it can obtain a higher return by reinvesting the funds.

Source: Ahli United Bank

6.7 APPENDIX 4: DEVON BANK

6.7.1   Residential *Ijara* Sale and Lease Transaction

An interest-free *Ijara* transaction provides more flexibility than some other forms of Islamic financing, but does involve additional costs and complexities. An *Ijara* transaction involves two components:

- a purchase agreement;
- a lease.

The customer finds the property he would like Devon Bank to purchase on his behalf. He negotiates the price and other aspects of the purchase and makes any initial payment of earnest money (a deposit) to reserve the property. The customer makes sure that the purchase contract allows Devon Bank to step into the transaction as the buyer.

The bank then buys the property. At the closing the bank enters into an agreement to sell the property to the customer for a fixed price – the purchase price the bank paid plus any transaction costs not paid by the customer at the closing. Ownership of the property is transferred to the customer after this price has been paid to the bank. A payment schedule is established so that in exchange for keeping the property rented, the customer's payments are deferred over time. These payments increase over time. The lessee, normally the customer, also pays the bank rent on the property the lessee is using but does not own. To the extent that the customer is making payments towards ownership under the purchase agreement, his rent will go down over time to reflect payments he has made towards the purchase of the property.

The transaction allows for recalculation of rent at periodic intervals over the time of the transaction. Part of the rent payment is tied to specific costs, such as taxes and insurance, and is adjusted annually. A second rent component is calculated based on an index identified at the beginning of the transaction, or it may be fixed long term. *Ijara* transactions make full or partial prepayments clear and easy to track.

All direct costs borne by Devon Bank (such as appraisal fees, taxes, recording costs etc.) are either paid by the customer at the beginning of the transaction or calculated into the rent.

Regardless of the religious accommodation underlying such a transaction, these transactions must comply with all applicable US Government regulations. For example, although structured as an interest-free transaction, Devon Bank is required to calculate a corresponding interest rate, and may need to disclose that rate to the customer in a government-required manner.

Source: Devon Bank

6.8 APPENDIX 5: MEEZAN 'EASY HOME' DIMINISHING *MUSHARAKA* AGREEMENT

6.8.1   Islamic Financing on a Diminishing *Musharaka* Basis

With 'Easy Home', the customer participates with Meezan Bank in a joint ownership of the property, known as a Diminishing *Musharaka*, where the bank will provide a certain amount of financing – usually up to 80%. The customer agrees to a monthly payment to be paid to Meezan Bank, of which one component is for the use of the home; the other component is for the equity share. The total monthly payment is reallocated regularly by the partnership to reflect the customer's growing equity and to allocate increasing amounts to the customer's investment. In fact the total monthly payment is reduced regularly as the customer's share in the property grows. When the customer has made the full investment, which had been agreed, the customer becomes the sole owner with a free and clear title to the property.

6.8.2   What makes 'Easy Home' *Sharia'a* Compliant and how does it Differ from a Conventional Mortgage?

As a Diminishing *Musharaka*, 'Easy Home' is *Sharia'a* compliant by conforming to *Sharia'a* laws specifically related to financing, ownership and trade. Taking ownership through a partnership and then transferring complete ownership to the consumer, instead of simply lending money, is the major factor that makes the product *Sharia'a* compliant. The nature of the contract is a co-ownership and not a loan because the transaction is not based on the lending and borrowing of money but on the joint ownership of an asset. Meezan Bank shares in the cost of the asset being purchased, for example, in this case for buying a home.

In conventional mortgages the interest charged is a mark-up on the money lent. The profit charged by Meezan Bank is the utilisation payment for the customer's use of the bank's share throughout the life of the contract. The profit is predetermined and based on market trends. Payments to Meezan Bank are hence completely interest-free.

6.8.3   Why is the Profit Margin Charged by Meezan Bank Correlated to Conventional Mortgage Market Trends?

At Meezan Bank the profit margin is directly correlated to market trends to provide a competitive product to their customers. *Sharia'a* allows the use of any conventional market factor as a benchmark to determine the profit rate of the particular product. The mere fact that the applied profit rate of the product is based on similar factors used in determining the applied rate of interest of a mortgage does not render the transaction or the contract invalid from the *Sharia'a* perspective, and neither does it make the transaction an interest-bearing one. It is the underlying structure of the product that determines its *Sharia'a* compliance.

6.8.4   Is the Profit Rate Variable or Fixed?

The profit rate used for 'Easy Home' is a combination of fixed and floating rates. The rentals for *Musharaka* property are calculated using a fixed rate applicable for the first year. The rentals are recalculated annually using a floating rate formula based on the average of 12 month Karachi Inter Bank Offer Rate (KIBOR) announced before the start of the calendar quarter.

6.8.5   What if a Customer Fails to Pay Monthly Instalments?

As far as the *Sharia'a* rulings are concerned, Meezan Bank cannot charge any penalty on the late payment but, to avoid late payments and instil a necessary culture of financial discipline, Meezan Bank are allowed, by their *Sharia'a* Board, to charge an amount that is donated to charity.

In the case of 'Easy Home', this amount is comprised of an upfront amount of Rs. 3000 when the payment becomes late with an extra 1% per day on the outstanding instalment payment. This amount is then transferred to the charity account managed by Meezan Banks' *Sharia'a* Supervisory Board.

Source: Meezan Bank

6.9   CASE STUDY QUESTIONS

1. What are the key principles underlying both conventional and Islamic home financing techniques?

    ✐ Conventional home finance _____

    _____

    _____

    _____

    Islamic home finance _____

    _____

    _____

    _____

    For Questions 2–9, you may like to use examples from Appendices 1–5 in your answers.

2. What is the role of profit versus interest in conventional and Islamic home financing transactions?

    ✐ Conventional home finance _____

    _____

    _____

    Islamic home finance _____

    _____

    _____

    _____

3. Who retains the title to the property in each transaction?

    ✐ Conventional home finance _____

    _____

    _____

    Islamic home finance _____

    _____

    _____

    _____

4. What are the *Sharia'a* rules as applied in the case of home finance?

_____

_____

_____

5. Outline the key characteristics of *Murabaha* as a technique for home finance.

_____

_____

_____

6. What are the differences between *Murabaha* and *Ijara* as techniques for home finance?

_____

_____

_____

7. Outline the key characteristics of *Ijara wa Iqtina* as a technique for home finance. How do the payment arrangements differ from those of a conventional mortgage?

_____

_____

_____

8. What are the advantages of *Ijara wa Iqtina* as compared to *Murabaha* as regards home finance?

_____

_____

_____

9. Summarise the key differences between conventional leasing and Islamic leasing.

_____

_____

_____

_____

10. Outline the key characteristics of Diminishing *Musharaka* as a technique for home finance.

    _____

    _____

    _____

    _____

11. Summarise the key differences between *Ijara wa Iqtina* and Diminishing *Musharaka* as techniques for home finance.

    _____

    _____

    _____

    _____

Case Study 7: Sources of Finance for Islamic Banks

7.1 LEARNING OUTCOMES

After reading Case Study 7 you should be able to do the following:

- Explain where Islamic banks get their money from.
- Describe an Islamic current account.
- Contrast the sources of finance of Islamic banks with those of conventional banks.
- Define a *Mudaraba* account.
- Define a Restricted *Mudaraba* account.
- Identify the concept of *Wadia*.
- Explain how *Mudaraba* works as a source of bank finance.
- Describe an Islamic savings account.
- Explain the concept of *Qard Hasan*.

7.2 WHERE DO ISLAMIC BANKS GET THEIR MONEY FROM?

Case Abstract

Conventional financial institutions operate as financial intermediaries, borrowing funds on the liability side of the balance sheet and lending funds on the asset side. In both cases 'interest' plays a pivotal role in the exercise. The *raison d'être* of Islamic banking, however, is derived from the Islamic injunction against *riba* (interest). Islam prohibits interest on deposits/loans regardless of their nature or purpose. This case study examines how, given that *riba* instruments are forbidden, Islamic financial institutions can operate as financial intermediaries.

7.3 SOURCES OF FUNDS FOR ISLAMIC BANKS

The sources of funds for Islamic banks are described in the following sections.

7.3.1 Current Accounts

All Islamic banks operate current accounts on behalf of their clients, both individuals and businesses. Current accounts are sometimes classified as 'other accounts' in the financial statements. These accounts are operated for the safe custody of deposits and for the convenience of customers. The main characteristics of these accounts are listed below:

- Current accounts govern what is commonly known as demand deposits. These accounts can be opened by individuals or companies, in domestic or foreign currency.

- The bank guarantees the full return of these deposits on demand and the depositor is not paid any share of the bank's profits, interest or a return in any other form.
- Depositors authorise the bank to use funds at the bank's own risk. Hence, if there is any profit resulting from the employment of these funds, it accrues to the bank, and if there is any loss, it is also borne by the bank.
- There are no conditions with regard to deposits and withdrawals.
- Usually account holders have a right to draw cheques on their accounts.

There are two dominant views within the Islamic banking community about current accounts. One is to treat demand deposits as *Amanah* (trust) accounts. This view is adopted by the Jordan Islamic Bank, which operates a 'trust account' instead of a current account.

The Jordan Islamic Bank defines a trust account as 'cash deposits received by the bank where the bank is authorised to use the deposits, at its own risk and responsibility with respect to profit or loss, and which are not subject to any conditions for withdrawals or deposits'.

These deposits are handed over to the bank by depositors, as a Trust, and the bank does not have the authority to use them without first obtaining the specific permission of the owner of the funds.

The other view is to treat demand deposits as *Qard Hasan* (interest-free loans). This view has been adopted by Iranian Islamic banks, which refer to current accounts as '*Qard Hasan* current accounts'. According to this view, money deposited in these accounts is a benevolent (or interest-free) loan from the depositor to the bank. The bank is free to use these funds at its own risk without any return to the depositor and without needing any authorisation.

In the case of *Qard Hasan*, the debtor does not need the specific permission of the creditor to use the borrowed funds. The debtor owes the creditor only the principal amount borrowed. This condition is fulfilled because the amount deposited in these accounts is fully underwritten by the bank.

7.3.2 Savings Deposits

Although all Islamic banks operate saving accounts, there are some differences in the operation of these accounts. A typical example is that of Bank Islam Malaysia, which defines savings deposits in the following way:

> The Bank accepts deposits from its customers looking for safe custody of their funds and a degree of convenience in their use together with the possibility of some profits on the principle of *Al Wadia*. The bank requests permission to use these funds so long as these funds remain with the bank. The depositors can withdraw the balance at any time they so desire and the bank guarantees the refund of all such balances. All the profits generated by the bank from the use of such funds belong to the bank. However, in contrast to current accounts, the bank may, at its absolute discretion, reward the customers by returning a portion of the profits generated from the use of their funds from time to time.

It must be pointed out that any return on capital is Islamically justified only if the capital is employed in such a way that it is exposed to business risk. If depositors with savings accounts are informed that the accounts are guaranteed, and that their amounts will be refunded in full, if and when they want them, as is the case with conventional banks, then, they are not participating in business risk. As such, those accounts would not be *Sharia'a* compliant.

Under these circumstances, it has to be made clear that savings depositors are not Islamically entitled to any return. If an Islamic bank refunds some portion of the profits generated from the use of saving deposits to the depositors, it is at the discretion of the bank concerned and it must be treated as a gift.

This is exactly the course of action adopted by Bank Islam Malaysia.

In contrast to this approach, Bahrain Islamic Bank calls savings accounts 'Savings Accounts with Authorisation to Invest'. Depositors provide the bank with an authorisation to invest their money. They have the right of withdrawal, but profits are calculated on the basis of the minimum balance maintained for a month.

Similarly, savings accounts at Dubai Islamic Bank operate as follows:

- Savings accounts are opened with the condition that depositors provide the bank with an authorisation to invest.
- Depositors have the right to deposit and withdraw funds.
- The profits in savings accounts are calculated on the minimum balance maintained during the month. Depositors participate in the profits of savings accounts with effect from the beginning of the month following the month in which the deposits are made.
- A minimum balance has to be maintained in order to qualify for a share in profits.

The Iranian Islamic banks include saving accounts in 'Qard Hasan Accounts' and call them 'Qard Hasan' deposits. The operation of these accounts is similar to that of savings accounts in the conventional system, as far as the deposit and withdrawal of money by means of a savings account passbook is concerned. Although no dividends are due, in the case of Qard Hasan depositors, Iranian banks use different promotional methods in order to attract and mobilise deposits. These include giving the following incentives to depositors:

- nonfixed bonus in cash or in kind;
- exempting them from, or granting discount thereto, in the payment of commissions and/or fees;
- priority to customers in the use of banking facilities.

In addition, Jordan Islamic Bank has adopted yet another way to operate savings accounts: it includes savings deposits in an investment pool called joint investment accounts.

To summarise, Islamic banks adopt one or more of the following practices when operating savings accounts:

- Accepting savings deposits on the principle of *Al Wadia* (trust), requesting depositors to give permission to the bank to use these funds at its own risk, but guaranteeing full return of deposits and sharing any profits voluntarily.
- Accepting savings deposits with an authorisation to invest and share profits in an agreed manner for the period in which a required balance is maintained.
- Treating savings deposits as *Qard Hasan* from depositors to the bank and granting pecuniary or nonpecuniary benefits to depositors.
- Accepting savings deposits as part of an investment pool and treating them as investment deposits.

7.3.3 Investment Deposits

Investment deposits are based on the application of the *Mudaraba* contract.

7.3.3.1 Mudaraba (Profit-Sharing Venture)

The *Mudaraba* contract is a contract between two parties whereby one party, the *Rab ul Mall* (the sleeping partner or beneficiary), entrusts money to the other party (the *Mudarib* – the working partner or managing trustee). The *Mudarib* agrees to use the money in an agreed manner and then return, to the *Rab ul Mall*, the principal and the pre-agreed share of the profit. The *Mudarib* is then rewarded with the pre-agreed share of the profit.

The following characteristics of *Mudaraba* are of significance for the sources of bank funds:

- The division of profits between the two parties must necessarily be on a proportional basis and cannot be a lump sum or a guaranteed return.
- The investor is not liable for losses beyond the capital he has contributed.
- The *Mudarib* does not share in the losses except for the loss of his own time and effort.
- The *Mudaraba* can be general purpose or for a specific purpose.

Investment deposits are Islamic banks' counterparts to term deposits or time deposits in the conventional system. They are also called profit and loss sharing (PLS) accounts, investment accounts or sometimes participatory accounts. However, they can be distinguished from traditional fixed term deposits in the following manner:

- Fixed term deposits in the conventional system operate on the basis of interest, while investment accounts in Islamic banks operate on the basis of profit sharing. Instead of promising depositors a predetermined fixed rate of return on their investment, the bank tells them only the ratio in which it will share the profits with them. How much profit each depositor earns depends on the final outcome of the bank's own investment.
- Although fixed term deposits are usually distinguished from each other on the basis of their maturities, investment deposits can be distinguished on the basis of maturity as well as other criteria. It is also possible to give special instructions to the bank to invest a particular deposit in a specified project or trade. These are known as Restricted Investment Accounts.

The main characteristics of investment deposits can be summarised as follows:
- Investment accounts can be opened by individuals or companies in domestic or foreign currency, provided that the bank is allowed to operate in foreign exchange activities.
- Deposit holders do not receive any interest. Instead, they participate in the share of the profits or losses, on a *Mudaraba* basis.
- Usually these accounts are opened for a specified period, e. g., three months, six months, one year or more.

The return on investment deposits is determined according to actual profits from investment operations of the bank and is shared in an agreed proportion by depositors, according to the amount of their deposits and the period for which they are held by the bank. As an accounting practice, the amount held in the account is multiplied by the period for which it has been employed and profits are distributed on a pro rata basis.

Generally speaking, depositors do not have the right to withdraw from these accounts as is customary with time deposits in conventional banks; however, withdrawals may be made under special circumstances.

Limited period investment deposits (unrestricted investment accounts)

These deposits are operated, inter alia, by Bahrain Islamic Bank and Kuwait Finance House. Investment deposits under this scheme are accepted for a specified period, which is mutually determined by the depositors and the bank. The contract terminates at the end of the specified period but profits are calculated and distributed at the end of the financial year.

Unlimited Period Investment Deposits (Unrestricted Investment Accounts)

These investment deposits differ from limited period deposits in that the period is not specified. Deposits are automatically renewable unless a notice of three months is given to terminate the contract. No withdrawals or further deposits are permitted in this kind of contract, but customers are allowed to open more than one account. The profits are calculated and distributed at the end of the financial year.

Specified Investment Deposits (Unrestricted Investment Accounts)

Some Islamic banks have developed an investment deposit scheme with specific authorisation to invest in a particular project or business. In this case, only the profits of this particular project are distributed between the bank and its customers, according to mutually agreed terms and conditions.

   In the case of specified investment accounts, Islamic banks function as an agent on behalf of depositors. One example is in the provisions of the Jordan Islamic Bank, which declares that the bank will accept cash deposits into specific investment accounts

> from persons desiring to appoint the bank as agent for investment of these deposits in a specific project or in a specific manner on the basis that the bank will receive a part of the net profits realised but without liability for any losses which are not attributable to any violation or default by the bank.

7.4 CASE STUDY QUESTIONS

XYZ Islamic Bank is an Islamic bank based in the Arabian Gulf. Tables 7.1, 7.2 and 7.3 contain three financial statements for the bank, respectively: income statement; bank liabilities; and profit-sharing ratios.

   For the financial data provided in the three tables, you are required to calculate the

1. Total returns to the bank.
2. Total returns to the investment/savings account holders.

Table 7.1 XYZ Islamic Bank income statement

Revenues	Dinars (millions)
Islamic financing	200,000
Operating expenses	
Salaries and benefits	10,000
Administrative expenses	10,000
Depreciation	5000

Table 7.2   XYZ Islamic Bank liabilities (PLS)

Investment deposit accounts	Dinars (millions)
One year deposits	13,000
6 month deposits	1400
3 month deposits	800
1 month deposits	400
Savings accounts	7900
Current investment accounts	1000
Total investment and savings accounts	24,500

Table 7.3   XYZ Islamic Bank profit-sharing ratios

Account class	Bank (%)	Investor (%)
1 year deposits	15	85
6 month deposits	20	80
3 month deposits	25	75
1 month deposits	30	70
Savings accounts	35	65
Current investment accounts	35	65

8

Case Study 8: Financial Statement
Analysis for Islamic Banks

8.1 LEARNING OUTCOMES

After reading Case Study 8 you should be able to do the following:

- Explain the sources of finance for a wide range of Islamic banks.
- Differentiate the major sources of finance for a conventional bank from those of an Islamic bank.
- Identify the major items on the asset side of an Islamic bank balance sheet.
- Identify the major items on the liability side of an Islamic bank balance sheet.
- Identify the major items on the income side of an Islamic bank income statement.
- Identify the major items on the expenditure side of an Islamic bank income statement.
- Calculate the appropriate financial ratios.

8.2 HOW DO THE FINANCIAL STATEMENTS OF ISLAMIC BANKS DIFFER FROM THOSE OF CONVENTIONAL BANKS?

Case Abstract

The financial statements of Islamic banks are very different from those of conventional banks. In this case, data is provided for a cross-section of banks from the Islamic banking world. You are advised to put this information into an Excel format, so that you can analyse the Islamic financial statements, drawing out the differences between them and those of conventional banks. You are then asked to analyse the differences between Islamic accounting statements within the different Islamic countries.

8.3 CASE STUDY ACTIVITIES

This case contains the balance sheets and income statements for the following Islamic banks, based in different countries:

- Shamil Bank of Bahrain (Bahrain): Table 8.1.
- Emirates Bank International (UAE): Table 8.2.
- Al Rajhi Banking and Investment Corporation (Saudi Arabia): Table 8.3.
- ABC Islamic Bank (Bahrain): Table 8.4.
- Jordan Islamic Bank (Jordan): Table 8.5.
- First Islamic Investment Bank (Bahrain): Table 8.6.
- Meezan Bank (Pakistan): Table 8.7.

- Investors Bank (Bahrain): Table 8.8.
- Al Baraka Islamic Bank (Bahrain): Table 8.9.
- Arab Islamic Bank (Palestine): Table 8.10.
- Bank Saderat (Iran): Table 8.11.
- Tadamon Islamic Bank (Sudan): Table 8.12.
- Amana Investments (Sri Lanka): Table 8.13.

Please note that the key issues here are the accounting principles rather than the years in which the accounts were prepared.

The principal elements in an Islamic bank's balance sheet are given below:

- *Assets:*
  - cash and cash equivalents;
  - participations;
  - *Murabaha* receivables;
  - *Mudaraba*;
  - *Musharaka*;
  - Investments:
    - Islamic securities;
    - Restricted Investment Accounts;
    - assets acquired for leasing;
    - other investments;
    - investment in commodities;
    - investment in securities.
  - *qard al hasan;*
  - other assets;
  - fixed assets;
  - total assets.
- *Liabilities:*
  - current account;
  - liabilities due to a financial institution;
  - investment by restricted investment account holders;
  - other liabilities;
  - total liabilities;
  - unrestricted investment account holders;
  - owner's equity;
  - share capital;
  - reserves;
  - retained earnings;
  - total liabilities and owner's equity.
- *Total liabilities, owner's equity, unrestricted investment accounts.*

Table 8.1   Shamil Bank Of Bahrain E.C.: Consolidated statement of financial position at 31 December 2000

	2000 $US 000	1999 $US 000
ASSETS		
Cash	310,751	358,535
*Murabaha*s	415,793	376,750
Investments		
Islamic securities	116,155	128,152
Restricted investment accounts	227,084	125,884
Assets acquired for leasing	41,723	49,908
Other investments	103,277	106,902
Other assets	89,035	103,940
Fixed assets	12,519	14,734
Total assets	1,316,337	1,264,805
LIABILITIES, UNRESTRICTED INVESTMENT ACCOUNTS, MINORITY INTEREST AND OWNERS' EQUITY		
Customer current accounts	64,729	47,377
Due to banks and financial institutions	89,366	117,660
Investment by restricted investment accounts	155,306	79,793
Other liabilities	76,819	45,839
Total liabilities		
Unrestricted investment accounts	682,152	730,653
Minority interest	15,445	12,566
Total liabilities, unrestricted investment accounts and minority interest	1,083,872	1,033,888
Share capital	230,000	209,000
Reserves	5195	24,602
	235,495	209,000
Treasury shares	(2685)	(2685)
Owner's equity	232,510	230,917
Total liabilities, unrestricted investment accounts minority interest and owner's equity	1,316,337	1,264,805

These financial statements were approved by the Board of Directors on 20 February 2001

	2000 $US 000	1999 $US 000
INCOME		
Income from unrestricted investment accounts	85,300	77,456
Less: return to unrestricted investments accounts	(72,823)	(74,369)
Group's share documents from unrestricted investments accounts as a *Mudarib*	12,477	3,087
Income from restricted investment accounts	85,332	104,123
Less: return to restricted investments accounts	(73,634)	(91,162)
Group's share documents from restricted investments accounts as a *Mudarib*	11,698	12,961
Total income from investment accounts (funds under management)	24,175	16,048
Income from Islamic financing and securities	18,202	16,763
Other income	5033	9873
Total income		

(Continues)

Table 8.1   (*Continued*)

	2000 $US 000	1999 $US 000
EXPENSES		
Administrative and general expenses	(29,773)	(28,405)
Depreciation	(2020)	(2815)
Total expenses	31,793	31,220
Net income before provisions and tax	15,617	11,464
Provisions	(5278)	(8786)
Overseas taxation	(1900)	6932
Net income before minority interest	8439	9610
Minority interest	(2416)	459
NET INCOME FOR THE YEAR	6203	10,069

These financial statements were approved by the Board of Directors on 20 February 2001

Table 8.2   Emirates Bank International, UAE: Group consolidated balance sheet at 31 December 2004

	2004 AED 000	2003 AED 000
ASSETS		
Cash and deposits with Central Banks	2,570,809	1,308,286
Due from banks	4,510,074	2,826,668
Property related receivables		
Loans and advances	27,036,401	289,333
Islamic financing and investment products	421,496	23,326,531
Investment securities	2,142,267	
Investment properties	172,455	1,874,663
Development properties		1,307,049
Fixed assets	179,231	212,112
Other assets	1,027,896	432,210
TOTAL ASSETS	38,060,629	31,905,128
LIABILITIES		
Customer deposits	19,138,703	20,543,571
Islamic customer deposits	1,233,654	
Due to banks	4,779,519	1,919,543
Deposits under repurchase agreement	355,087	355,087
Medium term borrowing	5,564,595	2,901,670
Other liabilities	1,169,223	670,654
TOTAL LIABILITIES	32,240,781	26,390,525
SHAREHOLDERS' FUNDS		
Share capital	1,435,014	1,148,011
Legal and statutory reserve	619,205	521,205
Other reserves	3,102,366	2,889,369
Cumulative changes in fair value	154,575	38,253
Retained earnings	505,288	362,863
TOTAL SHAREHOLDERS' FUNDS	5,816,448	4,959,701
Minority interests	3,400	554,902
TOTAL LIABILITIES AND SHAREHOLDERS' FUNDS	38,060,629	31,905,128
Interest income	1,198,819	943,793
Income from Islamic financing and investment products	1851	
Total interest income and income from Islamic financing and investment products	1,200,670	943,793
Interest expense	(380,444)	(275,429)
Distribution to depositors	(3145)	
Net interest income and income from Islamic products net of distribution to depositors	817,081	668,364
Fees, commissions and óther income	671,572	342,480
Property related income	110,496	99,430
Total income	1,599,149	1,110,274
General and administrative expenses	(606,003)	(493,519)
Net recoveries on advances	130	28,054
Share of profit of associate companies	40,377	4,059
Group net profit for the year before tax	1,033,653	648,868
Group net profit for the year before Minority interests	1,033,653	648,868
Minority interests	(61,526)	(31,051)
Group net profit for the year available for appropriation	972,127	61,781
	2004 (Dirhams)	Restated 2003 (Dirhams)
EARNINGS PER SHARE	**1.69**	**1.08**

Table 8.3   Al Rajhi Banking and Investment Corp., Saudi Arabia: Consolidated balance sheet at 31 December 2001 and 2000

	2001 SR 000	2000 SR 000
ASSETS		
Cash and precious metals	1,331,564	2,041,015
Deposits with Saudi Arabian Monetary Agency (SAMA)	2,736,688	4,418,443
Due from Banks	803,168	837.17
Investments, net:		
Mutajara	31,135,112	27,860,403
Mutajara by *Wakala*	459,525	3,879,213
Instalment sales	5,936,967	2,464,249
Istisna'a	3,959,737	4,437,113
Murabaha	692,816	706,037
Musharaka	47,733	56,258
Sundry, net	417,792	388.86
Total investments, net	42,649,682	39,792,133
Customer debit current accounts, net	855,246	788,131
Leased assets net	259,536	263,941
Fixed assets, net	768,678	691,792
Other assets, net	2,337,110	1,847,809
TOTAL ASSETS	**51,741,672**	**48,680,434**
LIABILITIES		
Customer Credit current accounts	37,800,900	34,442,929
Other customer accounts (including margins on letters of credit, third party funds certified checks and transfers)	1,683,473	2,207,950
Due to Banks	1,141,123	885,347
Proposed gross dividends	1,298,548	1,307,476
Other liabilities	3,097,409	3,360,001
TOTAL LIABILITIES	**45,021,543**	**42,203,713**
SHAREHOLDERS' EQUITY		
Share capital	2,250,000	2,250,000
Statutory reserve	2,250,000	2,250,000
General reserve	939,364	939,364
Retained earnings	1,280,765	1,037,357
Total shareholders' equity	**6,720,129**	**6,476,721**
TOTAL LIABILITIES AND SHAREHOLDERS' EQUITY	**51,741,672**	**48,680,434**
MUDARABA **FUNDS**	**7,355,061**	**6,469,913**
CONTINGENT LIABILITIES	**20,619,965**	**19,375,292**
INCOME		
Income from investments:		
Mutajara	1,584,454	1,740,744
Mutajara by *Wakala*	122,086	357,072
Instalment sales	585,576	231,341
Istisna'a	640,861	690,756
Murabaha	18,906	32,538
Sundry	3694	10,742

Table 8.3   (*Continued*)

	2001 SR 000	2000 SR 000
Total income from Investments	**2,955,607**	**3,063,193**
Leased assets income	25,140	27,632
Mudaraba fees	49,143	68,106
Exchange differences income	162,104	264,679
Other income	330,520	293,984
Total operating income	**3,522,514**	**3,717,594**
EXPENSES		
Salaries and staff related benefits	594,921	573,852
Rent and premises expenses	72,901	62,682
Provisions for doubtful accounts (Investments and other)	771,645	717,802
Depreciation and amortisation	164,732	139,102
General and other administrative expenses	373,635	322,171
Board of directors' remuneration	2724	2235
Total operating expenses	**1,980,558**	**1,817,845**
NET INCOME	**1,541,956**	**1,899,749**
Weighted average number of outstanding shares	45 million	45 million
Earnings per share	SR 34.27	SR 42.22

Table 8.4   ABC Islamic Bank, Bahrain

	2000 $US 000	1999 $US 000
ASSETS		
Cash and balance with banks	164	283
Due from Arab Banking Corporation (B. S. C)	20,978	22,343
Investment securities	14,941	14,459
Murabaha receivables	84,203	105,813
Ijara assets	37,711	43,058
Investment in a managed *Mudaraba*	309	46,100
Premises and equipment		
Other assets	1664	39
TOTAL ASSETS	**194,994**	**233,416**
LIABILITIES, UNRESTRICTED INVESTMENT ACCOUNTS AND EQUITY LIABILITIES		
Accounts payable and other liabilities	3372	3485
UNRESTRICTED INVESTMENT ACCOUNTS	135,973	176,960
EQUITY		
Share capital	42,500	42,500
Statutory reserve	2812	2415
	11,237	8056
	56,549	52,971
TOTAL LIABILITIES, UNRESTRICTED INVESTMENT ACCOUNTS AND EQUITY	**194,994**	**233,416**
RESTRICTED INVESTMENT ACCOUNTS	231,278	212,679
MEMORANDUM ITEMS	2060	2854
STATEMENT OF INCOME		
Income from investment securities	864	40
Income from *Mudaraba* receivables	8709	7835
Ijara income – net	2684	2581
Income from investments in a managed *Mudaraba*	1175	940
	13,432	11,836
Allocation to unrestricted investment accounts	(8423)	(6464)
Income attributable to the bank	5009	5372
Mudarib fees from managing unrestricted investment accounts	87	54
Mudarib fees from managing restricted investment accounts	1408	1095
Fee on restricted investment accounts as an agent	104	50
Other fees and commission income	605	1763
OPERATING INCOME	7213	8334
Staff costs	1678	1736
Depreciation	85	31
Others	1479	1637
OPERATING EXPENSES	3342	3404
NET PROFIT FOR THE YEAR	3971	4930

Table 8.5   Jordan Islamic Bank for Finance and Investment: Balance sheets as of 31 December 2001 and 2000

	2001 JD 000	2000 JD 000
ASSETS		
Cash on hand and at central banks	197,511	155,386
Cash at banks and financial institutions	91,918	104,657
Qard al hasan		
Murabaha, financing and investments		243,813
Murabaha receivables	228,325	12,049
Financing (*Mudaraba* and *Musharaka*)	11,964	16,434
Investment in commodities	35,581	36,869
Investment in securities	34,583	26,869
Investment in subsidiaries and associates	26,312	26,312
Investment in leases	3107	3295
Investment in real estate	21,656	25,576
Other investments	50,327	26,934
Total *Murabaha*, financing and investments	411,855	391,282
Less: Investment risk provision	26,901	24,976
Net *Murabaha*, financing and investments	384,954	366,307
Investment in securities – self financed	1973	2060
Fixed assets, net	15,965	16,839
Other assets	13,663	10,007
Total assets	709,588	658,892
Liabilities		
Banks and financial institutions current accounts	4550	4038
Customers current and savings accounts	146,670	16,383
Cash margins	12,670	11,066
Miscellaneous provisions	3231	3563
Other liabilities	20,203	20,293
Income tax provisions	113	825
Total liabilities	468,616	166,168
Unrestricted investment accounts and	468,616	438,195
Shareholders' equity		
Paid in capital	38,500	38,500
Statutory reserve	8025	7886
Voluntary reserve	920	643
Other reserves	2812	2812
Dividends	0	1925
Retained earnings	3322	2762
Total shareholders' equity	53,578	54,529
Total liabilities and shareholders' equity	709,588	658,892
Restricted investment accounts	126,505	117,941
Investment portfolios	71,352	51,431
Revenues		
Murabaha revenue	18,076,186	20,607,995
Financing revenue	362,199	379,630
Investment revenue	8,710,112	8,843,526
	27,149,097	2,831,151
Less: Return on unrestricted investment accounts	12,812,223	13,904,098
Investment risk provision	2,714,910	2,983,115

(*Continues*)

Table 8.5   (*Continued*)

	2001 JD 000	2000 JD 000
Bank's share in income as *Mudarib* and as fund owner	11,621,964	12,943,938
Add: Revenue from Banking services	2,341,814	1,959,175
Bank's income from its own investments	10,532	9,985
Bank's share in restricted investments profit as *Mudarib*	792,395	762,115
Bank's share in investment portfolio profit as *Mudarib*	253,315	67,500
Other revenues	1,158,232	1,114,995
Net operating revenues	16,178,252	16,857,708
Expenses -		
Employees expenses	8,466,547	7,993,364
Other operating expenses	3,889,782	3,540,090
Depreciation and amortisation	2,391,950	2,191,683
Miscellaneous provisions	47,000	92,578
Total operating expenses	14,795,279	13,817,715
Net income before income tax and fees	1,382,279	3,039,993
Provision for income tax	345,743	825,399
Jordanian universities' fees	13,830	30,400
Scientific research and vocational training fees	13,830	30,400
Employees' rewards		76,000
Board of directors remuneration	35,000	35,000
Net Income	974,570	2,042,794
Earnings per share	0.025	0.053

Table 8.6 First Islamic Investment Bank, Bahrain: Annual report 2001

Consolidated Balance Sheet	2001 US$ 000	2000 US$ 000
Assets		
Cash and balances with banks	3839	6218
Liquidity investment instruments	102,087	68,746
Short term investments	136,075	11,811
Long term investments	79,906	28,385
Account and notes receivable	80,115	70,346
Other assets	1878	996
Fixed assets	7225	6940
Total assets	411,125	193,442
Liabilities, Unrestricted Investment Accounts and Equity		
Liabilities		
Due to banks and other financial institutions	201,901	
Other liabilities	9350	7597
Total Liabilities	211,251	7597
Unrestricted Investment Accounts	37,804	45,985
Equity		
Share capital	112,500	112,500
Share premium	408	408
Statutory reserve	8131	4860
Retained earnings	21,948	10,842
Proposed dividends	16,875	11,250
Cumulative charges in fair value	2207	
Total Equity	162,070	139,860
Total Liabilities, Unrestricted Investments and Equity	411,125	193,442
Income from Investment banking activities	63,750	40,207
Liquidity investment instruments:		
Income earned	4582	3680
Income allocated to unrestricted investment accounts	1772	1043
Income allocated to restricted investment accounts	2810	2637
Murabaha expenses	5863	1648
Operating Income	60,697	41,196
Investment banking expenses	7346	2920
Staff expenses	12,376	8920
Depreciation	1618	1199
General and administration expenses	6646	7608
Operating Expenses	27,986	20,647
Net Income for the Year	32,711	20,549

Table 8.7   Meezan Bank, Pakistan at 31 March 2005

Unaudited Balance Sheet	Rupees in 000
ASSETS	
Cash and balances with Treasury banks	690,150
Balances with other banks	–
Due from financial institutions	1,524,348
Investments	14,120,765
Financings	1,013,532
Other assets	239,601
Operating fixed assets	22,551,463
LIABILITIES	
Bills payable	800,657
Due to financial institutions	2,848,320
Deposits and other accounts	15,547,555
Subordinated loan	–
Liabilities against assets subject to finance leases	–
Other liabilities	956,370
Deferred taxation	22,627
	20,175,529
NET ASSETS	2,375,934
REPRESENTED BY	
Share capital	1,697,152
Reserves	323,344
Unappropriated profit	315,309
	2,335,805
Advances against issue of right shares	–
Surplus on revaluation of investments	40,129
	2,375,934

Unaudited Profit and Loss Account	Rupees in 000
Profit/return on financings, investments and placements earned	239,778
Return on deposits and other dues expensed	113,461
Net spread earned	126,317
Provision against nonperforming financings (net)	35,805
Provision for diminution in value of investments	–
Bad debts written off directly	–
Net spread after provisions	90,512
OTHER INCOME	
Fee, commission and brokerage income	50,303
Capital gain on sale investments	100,264
Dividend income	20,453
Unrealised gain on held for trading investments	13,710
Income from dealing in foreign currencies	14,493
Other income	946
Total other income	200,169
	290,681

Table 8.7   (*Continued*)

OTHER EXPENSES	
Administrative expenses	142,491
Other provision/write offs	–
Other charges	74
Total other expenses	142,565
	148,116
Extraordinary/unusual items	–
PROFIT BEFORE TAXATION	148,116
Taxation – Current	2025
Taxation – Deferred	22,341
	24,366
PROFIT AFTER TAXATION	123,750
Unappropriated profit brought forward	191,559
Profit available for appropriation	315,309
Basic earnings per share	0.74

Table 8.8   Investors Bank, Bahrain at 31 December 2000

	2000 US$ 000	1999 US$ 000
ASSETS		
Cash and cash equivalents	3,199,446	2,215,526
Participations	34,969,883	34,757,786
Murabahas	875,000	1,625,000
*Mudaraba*s	2,543,420	3,754,754
Other assets	1,562,840	1,029,181
Fixed	248,216	164,145
Total assets	43,398,805	44,546,392
LIABILITIES AND OWNERS' EQUITY		
Liabilities		
Due to a financial institution	8,835,482	8,835,482
Other liabilities	352,941	2,544,508
Total liabilities	9,188,423	11,379,990
Owners' equity		
Share capital	32,913,333	300,000,000
Reserves	1,297,049	33,166,402
Total owners' equity	34,210,382	33,166,402
Total liabilities and owners' equity	43,398,382	44,546,392

These financial statements were approved by the Board of Directors
    on 14 April 2001

Statement of Income	2000 US$ 000	1999 US$ 000
Income		
Income from investments and *Mudaraba*	628,538	1,472,015
Dividend income	1,166,968	1,043,182
Fees and commission	1166	260,720
Total income	1,796,672	2,775,917
Expenses		
Administrative and general expenses	(1,358,513)	(1,064,282)
Depreciation	(21,132)	(7876)
Total expenses	(1,379,645)	(1,072,158)
Net income for the year transfer to retained earnings	417,027	1,703,756

These financial statements were approved by the Board of Directors
    on 14 April 2001

Table 8.9   Al Baraka Islamic Bank, Bahrain at 31 December 2001

Balance Sheet	2001 $US 000	2000 $US 000
Assets		
Cash and cash equivalents	47,518	27,917
Sales receivable	167,112	154,344
Investment		
Investment in *Mudaraba*	1000	1000
Investment in assets held for *Ijara*	8490	482
Investment in *Musharaka*	3377	2444
Investment in *Istisna'a*	1143	1401
Investment in Real-Estate	8793	8793
Investment in related companies	4935	4935
Investment in securities	5973	1719
Investment in managed funds	1948	2488
Total Investments	**35,659**	**23,261**
Leased assets	3964	9688
Fixed assets	1133	1341
Other assets	4200	3892
Total assets	**256,586**	**220,443**
Liabilities	24,278	
Due to central bank and other financial institutions	39,110	
Current and savings accounts	8018	
Other liabilities	71,407	
Total liabilities		
Unrestricted Investment Accounts	127,180	
Total liabilities and unrestricted investment accounts	198,586	161,379
Shareholders' equity	50,000	50,000
Share capital	4064	4275
Reserves	6936	4788
Retained Earnings	6936	4788
Total Shareholders' Equity	60,936	59,063
Total Liabilities, Unrestricted Investment Accounts and Shareholders' Equity	**259,586**	**220,443**
Restricted Investment Certificates	**58,637**	**75,784**
Commitments and contingent liabilities	86,854	75,784

Statement of Income	2001 $US 000	2000 $US 000
Income		
Income from deferred sales	16,671,241	12,050,338
Income from jointly financed investments	374,339	927,916
Total Income	**17,045,580**	**12,978,254**
Return on unrestricted investment accounts (Depositors' share of income)	(12,065,909)	(8,712,190)
Bank's *Mudarib* fee	1,002,770	569,485
Return on unrestricted investment accounts	**(11,063,139)**	**(8,142,705)**
Bank share of income from investment (as a *Mudarib* and as fund owner)	**5,982,441**	**4,835,549**
Bank's income from self financed investment	1,094,117	3,377,541
Bank's share in restricted investment profit as a *Mudarib*	57,363	1,180,099
Revenue from banking services	1,518,906	186,300
Other revenues	1,851,061	174,852
Total revenue	**10,503,888**	**148,159**

(Continues)

Table 8.9 (*Continued*)

Statement of Income	2001 $US 000	2000 $US 000
Expenses		
Operating expenses	(5,434,380)	(5,394,384)
Depreciation	(943,949)	(1,280,468)
Net income before provision and taxation	**(4,125,329)**	**(2,674,143)**
Net provisions for the year	(1,383,974)	(681,234)
Net income for the year before taxation	**2,741,585**	**1,992,909**
Taxation	(833,122)	(690,234)
Net income for the year	**1,908,463**	**1,302,685**

Table 8.10 Arab Islamic Bank, Palestine at 31 December 2002

Balance Sheet	2002 $US 000	2001 $US 000
Assets		
Cash and Balances at Banks	18,776	18,361
Cash at the Palestinian Monetary Authority	7971	17,264
Investment Instruments at Islamic Banks	22,959	28,652
Net Investment Activities	27,321	18,290
Charity Funds	3	6
Investment in Securities	8705	8726
Investment in Real-Estate	3545	3331
Net Fixed Assets	4441	4510
Other Assets	1341	1008
Total Assets	95,022	100,148
Liabilities, Unrestricted Investment Accounts and Shareholders' Equity		
Customers' Current Accounts	19,934	
Deposits due to Banks and Other Financial Institutions	3694	
Cash Collateral	1680	
End of Services Provision	380	
Other Liabilities	2297	
Total Liabilities	**27,985**	
Unrestricted Investment Accounts	**56,923**	
Shareholders' Equity		
Paid up capital	11,226	
Legal Reserves	152	
Statutory Reserves	274	
Fair Value for Accumulated Adjustments	1544	
Retained Earnings (losses)	(3082)	(2532)
Total Shareholders' Equity	**10,114**	**10,891**
Total Liabilities, Unrestricted Investment Accounts and Shareholders' Equity	**95,022**	**100,148**
Contract Accounts	**3708**	**6423**
Restricted Investment Certificates	**6750**	

Income Statement	2002 $US 000	2001 $US 000
Income		
Income from *Murabaha* Receivables and Investment Certificates	2719	2890
Less Return on Unrestricted Investment Accounts	(541)	(873)
Net income from *Murabaha* Receivables and Investments	**2178**	**2017**
Bank's share as a *Mudarib* from Restricted Investment Certificates	16	
Income from Bank's Services	802	316
Income from Investment in Securities	0	71
Income from foreign currencies exchange transactions	134	110
Income from revaluation of Investment in Real Estate	328	
Other Income	349	74

(*Continues*)

Table 8.10 (*Continued*)

Total Income	**3807**	**2589**
Expenses		
General and Administrative	3146	3378
Depreciation and Administrative	371	1180
Haj and *Umrah* Gifts	93	186
Provisions for Doubtful Debts	0	175
End of Services provisions	100	148
Bad Debts	163	13
Loss on Sale and Disposal of fixed Assets	17	8
Total expenses	**3887**	**5088**
Operating profit (loss) Before Tax and *Zakat*	**(83)**	**(2500)**
VAT – Previous Years	(374)	(141)
Zakat		(21)
Adjustments on Depreciation from Previous Years	(94)	
Operating profit (loss) After Tax and *Zakat*	**(551)**	**(2662)**
Retained Earnings	(2532)	130
Net income from (loss)	**(3082)**	**(2532)**

Table 8.11 Bank Saderat, Iran: Consolidated profit and loss account for the Iranian year ended 30.12.1379 (20 March 2001)

	Year Ended 30.12.1379 (20.03.2001) I.RLS	Year Ended 29.12.1378 (19.03.2000) I.RLS
Profit received		
Profit facilities	4,281,776	3,021,889
Profit on deposits and investments	359,423	266,560
Total profit received	4,641,199	3,288,449
Profit paid and prices guaranteed		
Profit paid	2,798,047	2,109,786
Cost of *Quarz al Hasaneh* prizes	53,513	42,818
Total profit paid and prizes	2,851,560	2,152,604
Net margin	1,789,639	1,135,845
Less:		
Provision for the bad and doubtful debts	(299,532)	(166,932)
Net Income (expense) generated from operations	1,490,107	968,913
Other income and expenses		
Net commission received	171,409	151,489
Net foreign exchange results	14,124	(2252)
Other income	338,011	343,074
Other expenses	(1,391,651)	(1,019,990)
Total of other income and expenses	(868,107)	(527,679)
Profit before tax	622,000	441,234
Tax	(62,346)	(195,357)
Profit after tax	559,654	245,877

Table 8.12   Tadamon Islamic Bank, Sudan: Consolidated statement of financial position at 31 December 2001

Assets	2001 $US 000	2000 $US 000
Cash and cash equivalents	6,506,083	4594
Bills purchased	4603	6551
	6,510,685	**4,599,659**
Deferred Sales Receivables		
Murabaha	1,334,509	1,297,947
Salam	64,195	981
	1,398,704	**1,298,928**
Investments:		
Musharaka	567,809	855,343
Mudaraba (Foreign investment deposits)	7,636,676	7,732,198
Participations (Share capital investments)	23,109	18,029
Other Investments	**1,107,893**	**124,628**
Total investments	**9,337,486**	**8,730,197**
Inventories	30,184	32,439
Other financing loans	142,926	67,084
Other debit loans	2,169,401	67,394,238
Fixed assets (net)	1,293,163	1,361,017
Total assets	**20,882,550**	**83,483,652**

Liabilities and unrestricted Investment Accounts holders	2001 $US 000	2000 $US 000
Bank payables	511,622	304,319
Saving and current accounts	8,425,346	5,465,258
Notes payable and certified cheques	498,747	653,478
Insurance	1,084,929	1,403,699
Other credit accounts	1,758,414	68,280,960
Total liabilities	**12,279,058**	**76,107,714**
Equity of unrestricted investment account holders	6,862,285	5,877,284
Total liabilities and unrestricted investment accounts holders	**19,141,343**	**81,984,998**
Shareholders' Equity:		
Paid-up capital	4974	4974
Statutory reserve	212,612	126,708
General reserves	158,090	82,374
Other reserves	476,560	
Capital reserves (Fixed assets Revaluation)	727,094	
Dividends under distribution		
Retained profits	161,876	
Total Shareholders' Equity	**1,741,207**	**1,498,563**
Total liabilities, unrestricted investment account holders and shareholders' equity	**20,882,550**	**83,483,562**
Contract Account:-		
Letters of Credit	5,513,028	5,128,997
Letters of Guarantee obligations	148,779	575,911
Investment Bills	797,856	575,911
	6,459,664	**5,843,605**

Table 8.12   (*Continued*)

Income from:	2001 $US 000	2000 $US 000
Deferred sales		
Murabaha operations profits	1,016,945	760,333
Salam sale profits		487
Income from deferred sales	**1,016,945**	**760,821**
Income from investments	89,577	75,368
Income from deferred sales and investments	**1,106,521**	**836,189**
Less:		
Return on unrestricted investment accounts before the bank's share as a *Mudarib*	(711,826)	(537,387)
Bank's share as a *Mudarib* (30%)	209,213	123,876
Return on unrestricted investment accounts	(502,613)	(413,511)
The bank's share in income from corporate investment	603,908	422,677
Income from banking services	624,097	502,861
Other Income	166,822	88,020
Total bank income	**1,394,827**	**1,013,558**
Administrative and general expenditures	(874,029)	(631,620)
Depreciation	(32,000)	(33,816)
Total expenditures	**(906,029)**	**(665,436)**
Total income	**488,798**	**348,122**

Table 8.13   Amana Investments, Sri Lanka for year ended 31 March 2000

BALANCE SHEET	2000 Rs. 000	1999 Rs. 000
ASSETS		
Cash in hand and Cash Equivalent	65,546	25,684
Investments in Certificates of Deposit	96,992	43,120
Investments in Real Estate	70,631	58,114
Amounts due from Subsidiaries and Associates	2516	6934
Investments in Subsidiaries and Associates	29,375	20,375
Loans and Advances	482,862	403,940
Taxation Refund Due	2877	
Prepayments and Deposits	12,504	3,663
Other Assets	73,114	11,393
Property, Plant and Equipment	34,757	21,803
	871,175	**595,027**
LIABILITIES		
Amounts due to Local Banks	96,992	43,120
Mudaraba Investments	543,680	338,331
Other Liabilities	22,647	28,979
Deferred Liabilities	478	252
SHAREHOLDERS' FUNDS		
Share Capital	205,200	184,680
Less: Preliminary Expenses	(2855)	(4441)
Retained Profit	5033	4106
	871,175	**595,027**
Commitments and Contingencies	131,127	85,272

INCOME STATEMENT	2000 Rs. 000	1999 Rs. 000
Total Income	70,149	50,445
Profit From *Mudaraba* Operations	69,623	48,773
Mudarib Share		
Profit Share of Investors	(38,350)	(20,216)
Net Profit From *Mudaraba* Operations	48,773	48,773
Other Income	48,773	48,773
Less:		
General and Administration Expenses	(26,721)	(18,208)
Loss on Sale of Plant, Machinery and Equipment		(146)
Preliminary Expenses written off	(1586)	(1586)
Profit Before *Zakat* and Tax	48,773	48,773
Zakat	48,773	48,773
Profit After *Zakat* and Before Tax	1491	7441
Taxation	(564)	(3)
	927	3991
Profit Brought Forward	4106	115
Unappropriated Profit to be Carried Forward	5033	4106

8.4 CASE STUDY QUESTIONS

Using the above financial statements, answer the following questions for each of the banks:

1. Define the main assets of an Islamic bank.
2. Break down the key assets into their major groups (calculate these as percentages).
3. Are the assets all treated identically in the accounts by the different banks? If not demonstrate the differences (*Ijara*, *Mudaraba* etc.).
4. Define the major sources of finance for Islamic banks.
5. Identify the key liabilities of Islamic banks (calculate these as percentages).
6. How important are current accounts and investment accounts as sources of finance?
7. Where, in the accounts, do you find restricted and unrestricted investment accounts?
8. Are investment accounts assets or liabilities?
9. Do the activities of the banks differ between countries?
10. How do the activities of Islamic commercial banks differ from those of conventional ones?
11. Do the Islamic banks featured in this case study make money?
12. Calculate the return on capital employed for each bank.

9

Case Study 9: Islamic Investment Prohibitions

9.1 LEARNING OUTCOMES

After reading Case Study 9 you should be able to do the following:

- Explain why Islamic investing is different from conventional investing.
- Describe the Islamic purification principles.
- Contrast an Islamic portfolio with a conventional portfolio of acceptable investment products.
- Define *zakat*.
- Describe the rules regarding the application of *zakat*.
- Identify who can receive *zakat*.
- Describe *riba* and explain its importance.
- Identify all the Islamic investment prohibitions.
- Explain the Islamic rationale for the ban on interest.
- Define *Sadaqah*.
- Distinguish *zakat* from *Sadaqah*.
- Define *Tamlik*.
- Explain the implications for *zakat* recipients of applying *Tamlik* principles.

9.2 MUSLIMS HAVE STRICT RULES ABOUT WHAT THEY ARE ALLOWED TO INVEST IN

Case Abstract

Conventional banking is secular in its orientation. In contrast, in the Islamic system, all economic agents have to work within the ethical system of Islam. Islamic banks are no exception. As such, they cannot finance any project that conflicts with the moral value system of Islam. For example, Islamic banks are not allowed to finance a distillery, a casino, a nightclub or any other activity prohibited by Islam or which is known to be harmful to society. The prohibitions, set out in the *Sharia'a* law, severely constrain the options open to investors seeking to invest Islamically. This is in stark contrast to the conventional investment options available.

All Islamic financial institutions, or institutions providing Islamic financial services, are obliged to have a *Sharia'a* Board to ensure these prohibitions are enforced. The prohibitions often do not involve simple *haram/halal* decisions: many investment choices involve combinations of *haram/halal* elements. This case study examines these prohibitions and highlights the complexities of dealing with the issues.

9.3   ISLAMIC INVESTMENT PROHIBITIONS

I heard Allah's Messenger say 'The *Halāl* (permissible) is clear and the *Harām* (forbidden)' is clear. Between these are matters that are doubtful. Most people do not know whether these are from the *Halāl* or from the *Harām*. So, he who leaves it (such matters) to guard his religion (against adulteration) and his integrity has indeed saved himself. He who engages (to any degree) into any of these (doubtful matters) would soon engage in the *Harām* just as he who grazes (animals) around (another's) territory is likely to enter into it. Be cautious! Each king has a territory. Be cautious! And the (prohibited) territory of Allah is His prohibitions.

Hadith narrated by an bin Bashir R. A.

Although the above *Hadith* has many applications in various areas of the *Sharia'a*, its application in finance is crucial because the earnings to be derived from Islamic investments are required to be strictly *halal*. Any products intended for sale to the Islamic community (*Ummah*) must adhere to the Islamic prohibitions on a variety of goods. So any products sold and/or invested in by Muslims must ensure that the products are not prohibited (*haram*) under the *Sharia'a*.

When there is doubt regarding whether Islam sanctions a specified product, it would be judicious to abstain from purchasing it/investing in it.

To take an example, gelatine is produced from particular products of cattle and pigs. (See Box 9.1 for details of some of the widespread uses of gelatine.) The position with regard to pork is clear; it is forbidden. With regard to cattle, things are not so clear. If particular cattle are not slaughtered in conformity with the *Sharia'a*, not only the slaughtered cattle would be classified as *haram*, but also any products derived from its meat, bones and fat would also be impermissible for Muslim consumption. Thus gelatine, produced from such cattle, would be *haram*.

Box 9.1   What is Gelatine Used For?

Probably best known as a gelling agent in cooking, different types and grades of gelatine are used in a wide range of food and nonfood products.

Common examples of foods that contain gelatine are desserts, jelly, trifles, aspic, marshmallows and confectioneries. Gelatine may be used as a stabiliser, thickener or texturiser in foods such as ice cream, jams, yogurt, cream cheese and margarine. It is also used in fat-reduced foods to simulate the sensation of fat in the mouth and to create volume without adding calories.

Gelatine is also used for the clarification of juices, such as apple juice, and of vinegar. Animal glues, such as hide glue, are essentially unrefined gelatine. It is used to hold silver halide crystals in an emulsion in virtually all photographic films and photographic paper.

In many cases there are few substitutes for gelatine, which creates problems for a *Sharia'a* investment adviser as regards how to handle the Islamic issues involved.

The ruling, regarding the slaughtering procedure, implies that any other products, containing such gelatine, could also be *haram*. Therefore, if a particular sweet company has used such gelatine in various sweet products then, for all such products, it would also become impermissible for Muslims to sell, consume and/or invest in a company making these products.

Gelatine did not exist in the prophetic period. Therefore, contemporary Jurists differ as to whether gelatine manufactured from non-*halal* bovine products and from pigs would be *halal* or *haram*. Gelatine is but one of many examples that could be cited.

The cautionary route to be adopted by an Islamic financing institution would be to abstain from financing, and or investing in, any sweet or other product containing gelatine that is not strictly produced from slaughtered animals that are classified as *halal*. The cautionary route may not be feasible business-wise, however, and may need to be tested with a *Sharia'a* board.

9.4   THE PROHIBITION OF INTEREST (*RIBA*)

The following *Hadith* on interest is of particular importance for Muslim investors:

> Ibn Mas'ud R. A. reported that Allah's Messenger S. A. W. cursed the eater of interest, him who fed it (to others), its two witnesses and him who recorded it.
>
> *Narrated by Tirmidhi*

Words in *Qur'anic* literature and the prophetic traditions (*Ahadith*) often have figurative meanings and care should be taken against misinterpreting them as having a literal meaning or, in some cases, to adopt a figurative meaning when a strictly literal meaning is intended.

Thus interest earned on money is not actually eaten but is used for a variety of financial requirements. In these narrations, the noun 'eating' is adopted instead of 'usage'. Most likely, any form of usage is equated in the *Ahadith* to physical eating, because although other forms of using interest may be external the religious harm or Divine punishment remains.

The *Qur'an* prohibits *riba* (interest), and *riba* is not to be considered to refer only to usury. Any loan in which the lender specifies a return in excess of the capital amount loaned is *riba*, irrespective of whether such an amount is moderate or excessive.

The forms of *riba* are not restricted to an excess over capital that is extended as a loan, as discussed below.

In the case of foreign exchange transactions, the failure to provide full reciprocal value in another currency, at the instance of the contract, is considered to be a form of *riba*. This is the case because it allows the party that has received payment/or the currency without providing the reciprocal exchange currency to benefit, potentially unjustifiably, from the money, by receiving interest in the time period prior to providing the reciprocal payment.

Capital owners are instructed directly to trade or invest their capital in Islamically permitted forms of investment and partnerships. Islam refutes the notion that capital providers can justify interest on the grounds that time has value; although money has a time value, it cannot necessarily be claimed that the passing of time always results in a profit to the providers of capital.

The Islamic prohibition against interest is so stringent that it even warns that witnessing or recording an interest transaction is sinful. Although the above mentioned *Hadith* literally mentions two witnesses, the number of witnesses is not limited. Therefore, even if a hundred or more persons witness an interest transaction, they would all be committing sin in the Islamic sense.

Islam declares, quite unequivocally, that acts of worship to Allah are unacceptable to Him if income, earned by worshippers, is from prohibited sources.

9.5 *ZAKAT* AND ISLAMIC PROHIBITIONS

Zakat is the Islamic concept of tithing and alms. It is an obligation on Muslims to pay 2.5% of their wealth to specified categories in society, when their annual wealth exceeds a minimum level (*nisab*). *Zakat* is one of the Five Pillars of Islam.

9.5.1 Who can Receive the *zakat*?

Eight categories of people may receive the collected *zakat*:

- Poor people (if they do not have enough to cover their basic needs).
- The Destitute (those with no property or income at all).
- The *zakat* collectors.
- People whose hearts are to be Reconciled, that is normally new Muslims or those close to becoming Muslim. However, even non-Muslims could be included.
- Persons freeing slaves.
- Debtors (to help those heavily in debt with paying their debts).
- Activities in the Way of Allah (running Islamic Schools, Hospitals, Mosques and other charitable works).
- Travellers (who find themselves in difficult circumstances).

9.5.2 How is *zakat* Connected with Islamic Prohibitions?

This issue is whether impure income can be purified by donating it as *zakat*, and if it can, who would be the appropriate recipients. The question that Islamic scholars debate is: 'Are the only appropriate recipients those falling within the eight *zakat* categories listed above?'.

9.5.3 Issues Regarding *zakat*, *Tamlik* and *Sadaqah*

One of the issues regarding payment of *zakat* is that of *Tamlik*, an Arabic term used by Muslim scholars that has been interpreted to mean 'complete and exclusive personal possession'. It means that when paying *zakat*, one has to hand it over to the exclusive possession of a deserving person. If accepted, the essential consequence of this interpretation is that while paying *zakat*, cash and goods can only be transferred to the personal possession of a poor or a destitute person: they cannot be handed over to an institution or a legal person. This complicates the position regarding the eight suitable categories for receipt of *zakat*.

Some scholars argue that *zakat*, via the *Tamlik* concept, is thus converted to a personal benevolence, which cannot be paid to institutions such as orphanages, schools or other welfare organisations. This rigid condition confines the social institution of *zakat* to an individual act of charity extended by one person to another. This mode of payment strips the institution of *zakat* of its social dimensions and effectively leads to the prohibition of *zakat* funds for nation-building projects.

The belief in *Tamlik*, as an essential condition for settlement of *zakat*, is backed by orthodox Muslim tradition, particularly by the *Hanafi* School of jurisprudence. The validity of *Tamlik* is drawn from the following verse of the Holy *Qur'an*:

> Alms shall only be for the poor and the destitute, for those that are engaged in the management of alms and those whose hearts are to be won in favour of the Faith, for the freeing of slaves and the debtors, for the advancement of God's cause, and for the traveller in need. That is a duty enjoined by God. God is all-knowing and wise.
>
> *Qur'an 9: 60*

The argument is based on the preposition *lam*, which is taken to connote *Tamlik* and has been used in the *Qur'anic* text for the first four categories of expenditure permitted for *zakat*, as mentioned in the above paragraph. It has been further argued that in case of the poor, destitute, those engaged in the management of *zakat* and those whose hearts are to be won in favour of the Faith, the preposition continues to extend the condition of personal possession. Thus *zakat* can be only paid by handing it over personally to all the deserving persons qualified under the four categories mentioned.

The doctrine of *Tamlik* leads to the following conclusions in relation to *zakat*:

- *Zakat* funds cannot be used for transporting alms from one place to another, because such expenditure does not qualify under the condition of personal possession.
- *Zakat* funds cannot be used to undertake projects of collective welfare of the poor. This exemption would include the construction of a mosque, school, library, dispensary, water supply scheme and lodging for the poor. Since these projects incur expenditure that is spread over a community of deserving people, the condition of personal possession is not fulfilled.
- *Zakat* funds cannot be used to meet the expenditure on the burial rites of a poor person because, after death, they cannot be made the owner of this money, in person.
- *Zakat* funds cannot be used for payment of loans outstanding against the deceased, for the same reasons.
- *Zakat* funds cannot be expended towards freeing a poor person in slavery because the money is to be paid to the master of the slave, and thus the condition that the poor person himself should get the funds in his personal possession first is not met.
- *Zakat* funds can only be paid to a poor person as a charity without any plan to enable that person to become self sufficient.

As a general rule no Muslim, by his free choice, should invest or deposit his money in an interest-bearing scheme or account.

If a Muslim has deposited money in an interest-bearing account for any reason, or the interest has come to his account without his choice or intention, he should not receive the amount of interest, but should surrender it to the payer of interest and/or donate the funds to a suitable charity.

In non-Muslim countries, however, it is permissible to receive the amount of interest with a clear intention that it will not be used for personal benefit. In this case it is incumbent upon the recipient to give this amount as *Sadaqah* to the poor who do not have the *nisab* of *Zakat*. This is not the normal *Sadaqah*, which a Muslim gives out of his lawful income with an intention to get reward in the Hereafter. Instead, this *Sadaqah* is meant only for disposing of unclean and unlawful money and to relieve Muslims from the burden of an ill-gotten gain.

But it should be remembered that this amount is unclean only for the person who has received it as interest. The poor persons who get it as *Sadaqah* can use this amount for their personal benefits. This amount can also be given to one's close relatives who are entitled to receive *zakat*. Even one's adult children can receive this amount if they are so poor that they can receive *zakat*, according to Justice Mufti Taqi.

It is important to stress that Islamic scholars do not all agree about many of these issues. Allah had made interest *haram* for all Muslims. To give poor Muslims interest is *haram*, unless, unless. . . .

9.6   CASE STUDY QUESTIONS

Muslims all over the world, despite all their commitment to Islamic values, face the problems brought before them by unwanted interest money generated in their name through channels they do not control. This happens, in spite of vigilance against whatever is likely to make them involved in interest-bearing activity.

In the event that interest does come into their accounts, no matter how unwanted, is there a valid way, under the *Sharia'a*, through which the identified amount can be disposed of?

You are asked to prepare briefs covering the questions below. It is not necessary to come up with definitive answers but some guidance is essential.

1. Would it be acceptable to finance food products whose ingredients are unknown?

2. Would it be the duty of a bank financing food production to keep a list of reputable and reliable institutions that are qualified to classify food products as *halal*?

3. What happens in the case of a client who contends that the religious school of jurisprudence to which he subscribes allows him to purchase, consume and sell products containing gelatine produced from non-*halal* sources? The argument here being that the religious school is of the opinion that the original material used to produce the gelatine is totally transformed within the production process?

4. Since the *Qur'an* prohibits assisting others in sin and evil, would an Islamic bank be allowed to finance the following:
   A Equipment used to produce wine, which also is used for nonalcoholic drinks.
   B Catering equipment for a company that primarily produces *haram* food products, which are to be sold to non-Muslims.

5. Can an Islamic bank finance an importer who wishes to purchase shoes with a pigskin lining, which are to be sold to non-Muslims?

6. Is it permissible to invest in a holding company when the Islamic status of the subsidiary company's income is unknown?

7. What should be done in regard to interest earned on accounts in cases where money had to be held in bank accounts, due to business or safety reasons?

8. Can interest income be used to pay taxes in non-Muslim states?

9. Can interest be used by the account holder or person who received it to pay other interest payments that are due, e. g., interest on a mortgage or other loan?

10. Can interest be used by poor Muslims who have no other sources of income?

11. Should interest earned or received be returned to the very same institution that provided the interest?

   _____

   _____

   _____

   _____

12. Should money be kept in the bank, for safety reasons, and thereby inadvertently earn interest?

   _____

   _____

   _____

   _____

13. What happens in the case of persons who are compelled to pay interest on loans, taken out to fulfil normal economic necessities, which are absolutely essential for the purpose of economic reasons or survival, e. g., buying a car or house on interest?

   _____

   _____

   _____

   _____

14. Would it be justified to buy a house on an interest basis when one can rent premises? What would the ruling be if renting the premises is not economically viable and the exorbitant rentals would prevent one from gaining the capacity to eventually purchase a property or other premises?

   _____

   _____

   _____

   _____

15. Can Muslims charge non-Muslims interest, when lending money, or are Muslims prohibited from charging everyone interest irrespective of race or religion?

   _____

   _____

   _____

   _____

16. Is interest only prohibited on loans for everyday daily spending or does the prohibition cover loans for generating further income using the finance for trade and investment?

_____

_____

_____

_____

17. What are the religious implications for Muslim accountants, lawyers and others who have to witness and record interest-based transactions?

_____

_____

_____

_____

18. Can a Muslim investment consultant advise non-Muslim clients to invest in activities where their income would generate interest?

_____

_____

_____

_____

19. Can Muslims buy assets, through interest-financing mechanisms, purely to minimise taxation?

_____

_____

_____

_____

20. Can interest earned on bank accounts be offset against bank charges?

_____

_____

_____

_____

21. Why should interest remain prohibited when it is well known that inflation eats into the real value of money?

_____

_____

_____

_____

22. Are any earnings acquired through the use of money borrowed on an interest basis, say through owning equities with debt in their balance sheet, also classified as prohibited in Islam?

23. Can a Muslim trade with another Muslim or non-Muslim whose earnings are from interest or other Islamically prohibited avenues?

24. What should a convert to Islam do in respect of previous earnings from interest?

25. Assume that a Muslim had earned interest from particular investments. He was ignorant of the fact that investing in particular portfolios also implied the earning of interest through specific financial instruments. What should he do subsequent to gaining awareness in this regard?

26. Can any earned interest be given to non-Muslim charities such as blood banks, heart associations, community service groups, welfare committees for the aged, sick and disabled, and similar other disadvantaged groups?

27. Are beggars on the street entitled to be given any earned interest?

   ✎ _____

   _____

   _____

   _____

28. Given that there are many non-Muslims earning very low incomes, would they be prefer-
    able as recipients of any earned interest?

   ✎ _____

   _____

   _____

   _____

29. Is it acceptable to give any earned interest to
    A Build toilets in mosques?
    B Help counter anti-Muslim propaganda in the media?
    C Build mosques?

   ✎ _____

   _____

   _____

   _____

10

Case Study 10: Opening an Islamic Bank Within a Western Regulatory Framework

10.1 LEARNING OUTCOMES

After reading Case Study 10 you should be able to do the following:

- Explain the key issues involved in creating an Islamic bank within a conventional banking framework.
- Describe the key principles distinguishing an Islamic bank from a conventional bank.
- Define the concept of *Sharia'a* compliance within the Islamic Bank of Britain (IBB).
- Contrast the profit sharing principles applied by IBB with the arrangements applied by conventional bank savings accounts.
- Define the role played by the UK Financial Services Authority (FSA) with regards to bank regulation.
- Identify the differences that distinguish an Islamic bank from a conventional bank with regards to the regulatory implications.
- Explain how the FSA resolved the key regulatory issues raised by the creation of IBB.
- Distinguish the banking products provided by IBB with their conventional counterparts.
- Explain the role played by IBB's *Sharia'a* Supervisory Board (SSB).
- Define a *Fatwa*.
- Describe the role played by *Fatawa* within IBB.
- Explain how the UK investor compensation scheme would work with an Islamic bank.

10.2 FIRST ISLAMIC BANK IN THE EUROPEAN UNION

Case Abstract

The creation of IBB was a pioneering event in the development of the Western banking system. IBB was the first fully-fledged Islamic bank to open in the European Union. It is important to appreciate the significance of this event given the differences between the conventional and Islamic banking models. The crux of the Islamic economic system is the sharing of profits and losses. All the liabilities and assets in the balance sheet of an Islamic bank are risk capital. In the conventional banking system, in contrast, the value of deposits is guaranteed by the bank, plus there is a guarantee of the payment of interest.

This case study examines the issues involved in opening an Islamic bank subject to a Western regulatory framework. The varied issues covered include nonpayment of interest, the differing banking products made available, the role of deposit protection and many other aspects.

10.3 ISSUES IN CREATING AN ISLAMIC BANK WITHIN A WESTERN REGULATORY FRAMEWORK

10.3.1 Background to the Creation of the Islamic Bank of Britain (IBB)

10.3.1.1 Authorisation of IBB

In August 2004, the Financial Services Authority (FSA) authorised the licensing of the Islamic Bank of Britain (IBB), the first wholly Islamic retail bank in a country where most of the population is non-Muslim. Inevitably, the process raised new questions and it took some 18–24 months to complete. The FSA was then able to carry over the lessons to later applications for banking licences.

The main issue that arose, in the licensing application, concerned the definition of a 'deposit'. In the UK, a deposit is defined as a 'sum of money paid on terms under which it will be repaid either on demand or in circumstances agreed by the parties'. This point is important because deposit-takers are regulated and the customer is assured of full repayment as long as the bank remains solvent. The savings account originally proposed by IBB as a 'deposit' was a profit and loss sharing account (*Mudaraba*) in which *Sharia'a* law requires the customer to accept the risk of loss of the original capital. This was not consistent with the FSA's interpretation of the legal definition of a 'deposit', which requires capital certainty.

After extensive discussions, the solution IBB adopted was to say that, legally, its depositors are entitled to full repayment, thus ensuring compliance with FSA requirements, but that customers have the right to turn down deposit protection, after the event, on religious grounds, and choose instead to be repaid under the *Sharia'a*-compliant, risk-sharing and loss-bearing formula.

10.3.2 The FSA's Approach to Banking Authorisation

10.3.2.1 The Financial Services and Markets Act 2000

Anyone seeking to conduct a regulated activity in the UK is required to apply to the FSA for permission under Part IV of the Financial Services and Markets Act 2000 (FSMA). The FSMA deals with the regulation of financial services in the UK and is the legislation under which bodies corporate, partnerships, individuals and unincorporated associations are permitted, by the FSA, to carry on those financial activities subject to regulation.

Under Section 19 of the FSMA, any person who carries on a regulated activity in the UK must be authorised by the FSA or be exempt. A breach of Section 19 may be a criminal offence.

10.3.2.2 Regulated Activities

The activities that are subject to regulation are specified in the Financial Services and Markets Act 2000 (Regulated Activities) Order 2001 (RAO). Examples include accepting deposits, effecting or carrying out contracts of insurance and advising on investments.

Before the FSA was established as the single financial regulator in the UK, several separate regulators oversaw different financial markets. The Bank of England, for example, was responsible for supervising banks under the Banking Act 1987 and the Securities and Investment Board was responsible, under the 1986 Financial Services Act, for investment regulation that was carried out by several self-regulatory organisations. However, under the FSMA, and subject to any specific restrictions, firms now seek a scope of permission from the FSA to be authorised for the full range of regulated activities they wish to undertake.

Most of the Islamic applications the FSA has received so far have been to establish Islamic banks. Banking itself is not a defined regulated activity; rather, the generally understood meaning is an entity which undertakes the regulated activity of 'accepting deposits' (and is not a credit union, building society, friendly society or insurance company). As defined by the RAO, this covers money received by way of deposit lent to others, or any other activity of the person accepting the deposit, which is financed, wholly or to any material extent, out of the capital of or interest on money received by way of deposit. This activity warrants classification as a credit institution under the EU Banking Consolidation Directive and firms undertaking it are subject to the appropriate capital requirements. A firm claiming to be a bank is therefore expected to seek this activity within the scope of its permission.

10.3.2.3 Nondiscriminatory Regime

All financial institutions authorised by the FSA and operating in the UK, or seeking to do so, are subject to the same standards. This is true regardless of their country of origin, the sectors in which they wish to specialise or their religious principles. This approach is fully consistent with the FSMA's six Principles of Good Regulation, in particular, facilitating innovation and avoiding unnecessary barriers to entry or expansion within the financial markets.

There is, therefore, a 'level playing field' in dealing with applications from conventional and Islamic firms. The FSA is keen to facilitate the expansion of Islamic finance in the UK, but it would not be appropriate, nor would it be legally possible, to vary its standards for one particular type of institution. The FSA's approach can be summed up as 'no obstacles, but no special favours'.

10.3.2.4 Authorisation Requirements

All firms seeking authorisation are required to provide a credible business plan and meet, and continue to meet, five basic requirements known as the Threshold Conditions. In summary, the five conditions are as follows:

- The firm must have the correct legal status for the activities it wishes to undertake. This recognises, for example, that European directives place certain limits on the legal form that a firm accepting deposits, or effecting and carrying out contracts of insurance, may take.
- For a firm incorporated in the UK, its head office and 'mind and management' must also be in the UK.
- If the person or firm has 'close links' with another person or firm, it must be the case that these are not likely to prevent the effective supervision of the firm.
- The firm has adequate resources, both financial and nonfinancial, for the activities that it seeks to carry out.
- The firm is 'fit and proper'. This takes into account its connection with other persons, including employees and shareholders, the nature of the activities it wishes to undertake and the need to conduct its affairs in a sound and prudent manner.

These conditions can readily be applied to any type of firm, although the exact requirements may need to be shaped to fit differing sectors. For example, the requirement for adequate resources, which includes capital, would be different for a bank as compared with an insurance company. However, the capital requirements for an Islamic and a conventional bank would be applied on the same basis. Another example would relate to the requirement that a business must have reasonable systems and controls to manage the type of business it wishes to undertake. In this case the threshold conditions are flexible enough to be as readily applied to an Islamic firm as to a conventional provider, whatever sector the firm is operating in.

10.3.2.5 Applying the FSMA

In applying the FSMA to Islamic firms, several areas need more work or clarification than would be usual for a conventional product.

The FSA has identified three main areas of potential difficulty that are common to Islamic applications: the regulatory definition of products; the role of *Sharia'a* scholars; and financial promotions.

Regulatory Definition of Products

The definition of products offered by Islamic firms is a key factor that firms and the FSA need to consider as part of the authorisation process. The structure of Islamic products is based on a set of contracts acceptable under the *Sharia'a*. So, although their economic effect is similar to or the same as conventional products, their underlying structure may be significantly different. This means that the definition of these products under the RAO may not be the same as the conventional equivalent.

This situation has two important implications for applicants. First, firms need to be sure that they apply for the correct scope of permission for the regulated activities they wish to undertake. This, in turn, highlights the need for firms to assess whether the structure of Islamic products can be accommodated within the RAO. Second, the regulatory definition is relevant in determining the framework in which products can be sold, for example in the application or otherwise of conduct of business rules. If a product falls outside the FSA's regulatory framework, there may be restrictions on who the product can be sold to. For these reasons, new applicants are encouraged to engage at an early stage with the FSA and their legal advisers about the regulatory definition of the products they intend to offer.

The Role of Sharia'a Scholars

The FSA also has to consider the role of the *Sharia'a* Supervisory Board (SSB). The industry defines the key objective of SSB scholars as ensuring *Sharia'a* compliance in all an entity's products and transactions. In practice *Sharia'a* scholars examine a new product or transaction and, if satisfied it is *Sharia'a* compliant, issue an approval (*Fatwa*). The FSA is, however, a secular and not a religious regulator. It would not be appropriate, even if it were possible, for the FSA to judge between different interpretations of *Sharia'a* law. However, the FSA does need to know, from a financial and operational perspective, exactly what the role of the SSB is in each authorised firm. In particular it needs to know whether, and if so how, the SSB affects the running of the firm. The FSA has to be clear as to whether the *Sharia'a* scholars have an executive role or one that is simply advisory.

This distinction matters for two reasons. First, in the UK, any person acting as a Director of an authorised firm must be registered under the FSA Approved Persons rules. To assess the suitability of a person, the FSA has a standard known as the 'Fit and proper test for approved persons'. One of the factors looked at is 'competence and capability'. So, for an individual to become a Director of an authorised firm, the FSA would expect them to have relevant experience. Therefore, if *Sharia'a* scholars are seen to have a directorship role, it is possible that some of them may not meet the competency and capability requirements.

Second, and assuming that *Sharia'a* scholars are directors, their role is more likely to resemble that of an executive director than a nonexecutive director, because it might involve active participation in the firm's business. In such cases, it would be very difficult to justify multiple memberships of SSBs of different firms because of significant conflicts of interests. This could put further constraints on an industry already facing a shortage of *Sharia'a* scholars with suitable skills.

From the FSA's perspective, the key point is that firms must successfully show that the role and responsibilities of their SSB are advisory and that the SSB does not interfere in the management of the firm. The firms already authorised have been able to demonstrate this. The factors that the FSA typically looks at with regards to SSBs include the governance structure, reporting lines, fee structure and the terms and conditions of the SSB's contracts.

On a related point, complex products, having gone through a long process of development, are sometimes rejected by the SSB for noncompliance with *Sharia'a*. To some extent, this situation arises as a result of the lack of *Sharia'a* knowledge internally in the firm. One solution put forward by some practitioners is greater involvement by *Sharia'a* scholars in the product development process. Although this may prove beneficial, it could lead to a more executive role as outlined above. A good industry practice, now developing, is that firms are starting to recruit more staff with an understanding of *Sharia'a* law. This could help to identify a product's potential noncompliance with *Sharia'a* at a much earlier stage.

Financial Promotions

The third issue, financial promotions, is more relevant on the retail side. Reflecting its statutory objective to protect consumers, the FSA's requirement is that all advertising should be 'clear, fair and not misleading'. This has been important in the context of Islamic finance because the products are still new and their structures differ from more conventional products. Together with the fact that by necessity those who wish to use them may be relatively inexperienced in financial services, this requirement reinforces the need for the promotion of Islamic financial products to include the risks as well as the benefits.

The following discussion shows how IBB dealt with these issues in practice.

10.3.3   IBB and the FSA

A working group chaired by the late Eddie George (formerly the Governor of the Bank of England) considered the barriers to Islamic mortgages in the United Kingdom. The greatest barrier appeared to be the fact that Islamic mortgages attracted stamp duty on the purchase of the property by the bank and on the transfer of the property by the bank to the customer at the end of the mortgage term. The FSA therefore welcomed the UK government's reform in 2003, which made stamp duty payable only once.

All firms who wish to carry out a regulated financial service in the UK must obtain FSA authorisation. The process can be quite lengthy with applications taking up to six months once the FSA has received the formal application. Any application for authorisation to the FSA, whether by a conventional or an Islamic bank, requires a credible and well thought out business plan. Applicants are expected to have conducted proper market research to assess the market appetite for their products as well as the risks such products present to consumers. The FSA was conscious that IBB's application for authorisation was the first Islamic banking application in the United Kingdom but, crucially, was able to be flexible within the confines of its own rules.

10.3.3.1 Issues Addressed

The FSA identified five specific issues arising in the context of Islamic banking:

- Risks in Islamic operations.
- FSA's definition of 'deposits'.
- *Sharia'a* compliance and the role of the SSB, a body unique to Islamic firms.
- Regulation of Islamic products, such as Islamic mortgages.
- Corporate governance in Islamic firms.

Risks in Islamic Operations

There are added risks and complications in Islamic banking caused by the need to ensure full *Sharia'a* compliance at all times. The FSA recognised such risks but did not consider them to be so substantial that they would prevent authorisation. The FSA needs only to be satisfied that an Islamic bank has taken all necessary steps to mitigate such risks.

FSA's Definition of 'Deposits'

The main issue arising in the context of Islamic banking is the definition of 'deposits'. In the UK, a 'deposit' is defined as a 'sum of money paid on terms under which it will be repaid either on demand or in circumstances agreed by the parties'. Therefore, deposit-takers are regulated and the customer is assured full repayment provided that the bank remains solvent.

The FSA's interpretation, in line with other developed legal systems, requires capital certainty. Unless the bank is actually insolvent it must return the customer's original money to him in full together with the return earned on it. However, if capital certainty is not assured, the bank is subject to more extensive obligations to treat customers fairly and to explain how the product operates.

The FSA had to categorise the following two types of Islamic savings accounts as either 'deposits' or 'investments':

- a simple noninterest bearing account, where the bank promises capital repayment; and
- a profit and loss sharing account (*Mudaraba*) where *Sharia'a* law requires that the customer accepts the risk of loss of his original capital.

Islamic banks prefer their profit and loss sharing accounts to be treated as 'deposits' so that they are in a position to compete with conventional banks.

In the case of IBB's product, the solution for the bank was to offer its customer full repayment of the investment, thus ensuring full compliance with the legal definition of a deposit. However, the bank calculates the amount of the repayment to comply with the risk-sharing formulation and the customer need not accept repayment in full.

Islamic Complications

Islamic principles of finance can produce surprises for regulators. Straightforward current accounts (chequing accounts) provided by banks are sufficiently well established in the lexicon of Islamic finance for such accounts to be uncontentious. They are intrinsically *Sharia'a* compliant. The same cannot be said to be true of bank deposit accounts. From a *Sharia'a* perspective, the customer needs to be sharing risk with the bank. From a UK bank deposit perspective such an arrangement cannot constitute a bank deposit, because it is inimical to the statutory scheme for protecting bank deposits for customers to be exposed to any form of risk (certainly up to the cut-off point for protection under the bank deposit protection scheme).

The FSA had to determine whether this product should be treated as an investment management agreement rather than as a bank deposit. From IBB's perspective, there was a substantial preference for the product to be treated as a bank deposit, because it would more sensibly complement the other products in IBB's launch range of banking services. For such an instrument to be treated as a bank deposit, the FSA insisted that it must have the characteristics of a bank deposit as they are defined in subordinate legislation under the FSMA.

Article 5 of the Financial Services and Markets Act 2000 (Regulated Activities) Order 2001 (as amended) states, in paragraph (2) that

> ...'deposit' means a sum of money... paid on terms
>   (a) under which it will be repaid, with or without interest or premium, and either on demand or at a time or in circumstances agreed by or on behalf of the person making the payment and the person receiving it ...

The unconditional nature of the repayment obligation is a key feature of what constitutes a bank deposit in the UK. Conditionality through risk sharing, however, is key to the *Sharia'a* notion of a 'deposit'. IBB's terms for deposit accounts contain a provision (Paragraph 6, see below) that successfully synthesises the FSA position on what properly constitutes a bank deposit and the position adopted by *Sharia'a* scholars on the pure nature of such a saving arrangement.

Paragraph 6 (in full) reads as follows:

> 6.1: It is a *Sharia'a* principle that profit-and-loss sharing accounts such as the savings and term deposit account involve (1) the potential for your capital to make a profit for you and (2) the risk that your capital could suffer loss, in the event of the pooled funds administered by us returning a loss.
>
> 6.2: When your capital makes a profit we shall account to you for that profit in accordance with these special conditions.
>
> 6.3: As a matter of English law (which applies to these special conditions) and in accordance with our Memorandum and Articles of Association, in the event that your capital suffers a loss, we shall seek to mitigate the loss in the following manner:
>
> 6.3.1: we may forego some or all of the fees chargeable by us in respect of the investment of the pooled funds for the calculation period relevant to your account(s).
>
> 6.3.2: we shall draw upon any available balance in the profit stabilisation reserve account administered by us to make good as much of your capital loss as the available balance permits us to do.
>
> 6.3.3: in accordance with our Memorandum and Articles of Association, our directors are prevented from declaring any distribution to our shareholders unless they are satisfied that there is no shortfall in meeting your claim(s).

6.4: If the pooled funds referable to your capital return a loss, we shall make an offer to you to make good the amount of any shortfall that you may have suffered. We are required by current UK bank regulations and policy to make this offer to you. If you choose to accept this offer, you shall be entitled to receive payment from us of the full amount that you had previously deposited with us. You are entitled to refuse this offer from us.

6.5: We would like to draw your attention to the guidance offered by our *Sharia'a* Supervisory Board. Their guidance is that if you accept our offer to make good the amount of any shortfall (set out in special condition 6.4), you will not be complying with *Sharia'a* principles.

6.6: In certain circumstances we may not be able to pay back to you the amount that we are obliged under these terms and conditions to pay back to you. If the terms of the Financial Services Compensation Scheme (FSCS) apply in these circumstances you may be able to apply to the FSCS for payment of compensation.

6.7: If you have suffered a loss in respect of which we have made an offer to you which you have accepted (see special condition 6.4), you may be able to apply successfully to the FSCS for payment of compensation if we fail to make payment to you in respect of that loss. If you have refused such an offer from us, you may not be able to apply successfully to the FSCS for payment of compensation in respect of the amount that was previously refused by you.

6.8: Should you suffer a capital loss due to fraud, gross misconduct or gross negligence committed by us, then we may be obliged, in accordance with *Sharia'a* principles, to make good to you any such capital loss on your savings or term deposit account out of money held by us on behalf of our shareholders.

Source: IBB

Sharia'a *Compliance and the Role of the SSB*

The FSA is a financial, not a religious regulator, and it is not responsible for ensuring that a product offered is in compliance with *Sharia'a* law.

Islamic banks must establish clear policies on *Sharia'a* compliance and its independent monitoring. Usually, both internal and external auditors are involved in monitoring *Sharia'a* compliance. However, UK accountants are not generally expected to be *Sharia'a* experts. It is therefore practical, the FSA argued, to appoint internal auditors who have a good grounding in Islamic law in order to monitor *Sharia'a* compliance.

The FSA also had to obtain an understanding of the SSB's role in an Islamic bank from both a financial and operational perspective. If the SSB's role corresponded to that of a director in a conventional bank, the individuals on the board would have to be approved by the FSA.

Sharia'a-*Compliant Accounting Practices*

The FSA attaches great importance to the integrity of accounting practices within financial institutions, the timely provision of management information within financial institutions and the cooperation of an institution's management with its external auditors on those occasions where external auditors are seeking to understand the nature of the company in question. From the outset, the promoters of IBB informed the FSA that *Sharia'a*-compliant accounting practices would have to be used in order to ensure product integrity from a *Sharia'a* perspective. If a product, from a *Sharia'a* perspective, entails risk sharing by the customer and by the bank, the accounting must reflect this fact.

The Role of the Sharia'a *Supervisory Board (SSB)*

The Islamic financial institution's board of *Sharia'a* scholars is something of a curiosity for many observers. *Sharia'a* Supervisory Boards have policies and procedures, undertake formal meetings and, with the right level of assistance, will produce written notes of relevant parts of their proceedings. Such SSBs are as likely to meet outside the UK as they are inside it. The SSB has the right to seek views from whomsoever it sees fit and to ask questions of a bank's management and directors. There is an informality and flexibility around SSB proceedings that appeals to the FSA.

Provided that a bank's management ensures that the proceedings are suitably documented and, when an issue emerges, the resolution of it is properly documented, then it appears to be the case, the FSA reasons, that the onus of running a SSB falls upon a bank's management, as opposed to anyone else. The members of a SSB will be well versed in *Sharia'a* law. *Sharia'a* scholars cover many different issues under *Sharia'a* law, which inevitably makes a number of them more generalised in nature than is the case with specialist finance lawyers practising within other legal jurisdictions.

Regulation of Islamic Products

The FSA did not view it necessary to regulate Islamic products on the wholesale market (on which historically much activity has focused in the UK). Thus, Islamic instruments traded on the wholesale markets, such as *sukuk* and *Murabaha* contracts, were not regulated in the United Kingdom. However, the banks that traded Islamic instruments were regulated.

Whether Islamic products are sold by Islamic or conventional banks, the FSA generally does not wish to intervene on the market unless there is a market failure or if one party (usually the firm) has much more information than the other (the consumer).

Corporate Governance

The FSA identified some serious and largely unresolved corporate governance issues within the 'classic' Islamic banking model.

The first issue is that Islamic banks wish to provide a steady rate of return to their 'investment account holders' – that is profit and loss sharing savers – by creating reserves to smooth fluctuations, and such reserves are placed in profit equalisation accounts or investment reserve accounts. But such accounts create an inherent conflict by favouring one class of investor over another – for example, investment account holders over shareholders, or present investment account holders over future investment account holders – unless there are tight, unambiguous and prescriptive rules as regards the amounts to be placed into such accounts.

The second issue is the treatment of investment account holders themselves within the corporate governance structure. Investment account holders share in the fortunes of the bank in a way that the traditional depositors do not. Despite this right, investment account holders do not have an automatic right to representation in the corporate governance structure. Shareholders consider that investment account holders should not be entitled to influence how the business is run or its strategic direction. Yet, investment account holders are vulnerable to a range of risks, such as insider dealing (an employee of the bank obtains information as regards a bad loan that may result in a loss to the investment account holders). In addition, investment account holders earn their return on the date of the calculation of such return, and in the event that returns are diverted into or out of profit equalisation accounts to smooth fluctuations, investment account holders may actually be gaining or losing at the expense of past or future investment account holders.

These risks also arise within the conventional securities and mutual fund industries. However, they are well understood by market players and regulations are in place, for example, to prevent insider dealing. To date, no such regulation has been implemented in the Islamic banking industry.

Overall, the prudential Basel framework is helpful in understanding and mitigating risks arising in Islamic banking, but the FSA believes that the framework is insufficient and investment account holders are best protected by means of securities-type regulations. Islamic banks themselves need to recognise these risks and establish internal policies to deal with such conflicts. Islamic banks should consider instituting a corporate governance structure that embeds protection of investment account holders, the FSA reasons.

The FSA believes that the conflicts considered above must be openly aired and understood at the level of the board of directors, and the board must set a clear and detailed framework for resolving them.

Composition of the Board of Directors

Given that corporate governance structures are generally designed to protect shareholders' interests, should the board have an independent member to protect the interests of the investment account holders? In IBB's case, the FSA did not impose a disclosure regime for the protection of the investment account holders, or insist on the appointment of an independent board member to protect the interests of investment account holders. However, IBB has structured its Islamic savings products to ensure that it is capital certain.

The FSA's concern with respect to the board of directors is to ensure a sufficient number of independent nonexecutive directors with relevant financial services experience. In the IBB case, the FSA was concerned that the independent nonexecutive directors should have UK retail banking experience. Experience of a *Sharia'a*-compliant institution was a much less vital consideration for the FSA. This is partly explained by understanding the role that the SSB must adopt within any financial institution that wishes to be *Sharia'a* compliant or to have an Islamic window. The Islamic Bank of Britain, naturally enough, has a SSB comprising three scholars. In addition to the focus on having independent nonexecutive directors (at least two is the minimum stipulation), the FSA was concerned to understand the antecedents of every other director.

Each of the other directors was seen as being affiliated in one of two ways: either (i) the director is a member of the executive management team or (ii) a major shareholder wished to see that person on the board of directors. At this stage, it becomes readily apparent that the executive management team has to have conviction and confidence if it is to lead the company forward when, on the board, there may be individuals who have a substantially different perspective on the bank and its future.

Ownership

The FSMA provides that anyone who holds 10% or more of an entity that is, or wishes to be, authorised by the FSA will be treated as a controller of that entity. The FSA is entitled to approve, or disapprove, a person or connected persons who constitute a controller. This becomes an important consideration when financing a start-up operation. Parties who are interested in financing such a project may have no interest in succumbing to the due diligence requirements that are all part of being a controller.

In the case of IBB, this was an important consideration. Potential investors were fully informed that in contributing to the pre-authorisation financing of IBB, it was possible that the firm would not be successful in its quest to obtain a banking licence from the FSA. In such circumstances, it would be highly likely that such investors would see no return on their investment and might receive back less than they had invested. To then have to submit to the due diligence requirements associated with controller status would be unattractive for many such investors.

In the pre-authorisation phase, and needing to finance the costs of progressing the project to the point where it obtained FSA authorisation, IBB promoters carried out a private placement of shares in IBB, largely in the Middle East, in order to raise pre-FSA authorisation financing. They were successful in raising the amount that they judged necessary to take the project to the next stage: applying for, and being successful in obtaining, FSA authorisation for IBB and its business plan. In carrying out the private placement, the promoters of IBB were conscious that enthusiastic investors should be advised of the controller requirement and, in addition, investors needed to understand the nature of connected party provisions that could deem more than one person to be constituting a controller when deemed to be acting in concert with other parties. In IBB's case, a tiny number of investors were prepared to assume the mantle of controller status.

When the FSA was wrapping up its consideration of IBB's authorisation application in 2004, it was fully aware that, following the granting of authorisation, IBB would move forward rapidly with a second capital raising and seek admission to the Alternative Investment Market (AIM) operated by the London Stock Exchange. The second capital raising was completed in October 2004.

IBB now offers a range of retail and business banking services. It has established eight branches in UK cities with large Muslim populations, around the country. According to recent figures, the bank had over 50,000 accounts and some 48,000 customers.

10.3.4   Islamic Financial Products Offered by IBB

10.3.4.1   Banking with Sharia'a Principles

The principles of *Sharia'a* prohibit the charging or receiving of interest, therefore all IBB's accounts are founded on a mutually agreed sharing of profit. Instead of charging or paying the customer interest, IBB undertakes only *Sharia'a*-compliant financing and investments. Depending on the type of account the customer holds with IBB, it shares profits with them.

As a stand-alone bank, IBB makes every effort to ensure that it does not compromise the principles of the Islamic faith. IBB never deals in alcohol, tobacco, gold or silver, or mixes IBB's funds with interest-bearing funds.

10.3.4.2   IBB Current Account

Pay no interest, receive no interest!

The IBB *Sharia'a*-compliant current account takes care of the essentials, offering banking services that the customer would expect from a high street bank without compromising the customers' principles. The IBB current account pays the customer no interest and the customers pay no interest to IBB.

IBB use the Islamic principle of *Qard* for their current accounts: a *Qard* is a loan, free of profit. In essence, it means that the customer's current account is a loan to the bank, which is used by the bank for investment and other purposes. Obviously it has to be paid back to the customer, in full, on demand.

It allows customers the peace of mind when depositing their money in a bank, with the additional reassurance that the Islamic Bank of Britain is not investing their money in activities that contravene *Sharia'a* principles.

Like all IBB accounts, the current account has been approved by the IBB *Sharia'a* Supervisory Board. Some of the features and benefit of the IBB current account are as follows:

- A cheque book and multi-functional bank card is offered, allowing customers to withdraw and spend money at their convenience:
- It is an interest-free bank account: receives no interest, pays no interest.
- A debit card and cheque book is offered with £50 cheque guarantee facility (or cash card – subject to status).
- Deposits may be made by cash, cheque or direct account transfer.
- Withdrawal of funds are available at IBB branches through an ATM, or by direct account transfer to another bank account.
- Funds deposited are administered in accordance with *Sharia'a* principles.
- It offers standing order and direct debit facilities.
- Regular statements are provided (frequency is subject to the account type).
- International payments are available.
- Access to IBB foreign currency and travellers' cheque services is offered.
- Automatic access to the customer's account is available via IBB automated telephone banking service 24/7 or online.

10.3.4.3 IBB Islamic Savings Account

The IBB savings account is run according to the Islamic financial principles of *Mudaraba*. IBB uses the customer's money to generate a profit, which then will be shared with the customer according to the profit sharing ratio on the customer account.

So, the more profit IBB makes with the customer's money the more the customer gets in return. Every month IBB announce its target rates for each of its savings accounts. This information is available in the IBB branches, on the IBB website and via the IBB telephone banking service. IBB normally achieves the target rates it advertises (see Table 10.1).

The IBB *Sharia'a*-compliant savings account lets customers profit from their savings while remaining true to Islamic principles. IBB does not offer customers interest on their funds. Instead it undertakes *Sharia'a*-compliant activities with the intention of generating profit, which it then shares with customers.

Table 10.1 Savings rate for the month of October 2007

Product	Target rate (%)	Achieved rate (%)
Undetermined term: 'savings account'	2.00	2.20
Young persons savings account	2.50	2.50
Direct savings account	3.00	3.00
Fixed term deposit 30 days (1 month)	3.25	3.25
Fixed term deposit, 90 days to 180 days	3.50	3.50
Fixed term deposit, minimum 180 days (6 months)	3.75	3.75

As well as being in accordance with the *Sharia'a*, the IBB savings account offers complete transparency with bank charges and customers may make cash withdrawals from their accounts at any of IBB branches without penalty and with no notice required. IBB's aim is to offer the customer a fair deal.

The IBB savings account is operated under *Mudaraba* principles.

What is Mudaraba?

Mudaraba refers to an investment on behalf of the customer by a more professional investor. It takes the form of a contract between two parties: one provides the funds and the other provides the expertise, and they agree in advance to the division of any profits made. In other words, IBB would make *Sharia'a*-compliant investments and share the profits with the customer, in effect charging for the time and effort. If no profit is made, the loss is borne by the customer and the Islamic Bank of Britain takes no fee.

Profit Rates

Although IBB investment methods are strictly in keeping with the *Sharia'a*, the bank makes every effort to ensure that the profit rates paid on all IBB savings accounts are market-competitive.

Profit Sharing Ratio

For savings accounts the customer's share of profit is paid on the calculation date, and for term deposit accounts it is paid on the maturity date of that deposit.

The following deductions are made in calculating the customer's share of profit for a calculation period:

- Operating fees and expenses: direct costs, fees and expenses are limited to 1.5% of the average pooled funds during the calculation period.
- Profit stabilisation reserve contribution: deduction from net income for this contribution is limited to 20% of the net income.
- IBB's share of profit.

The percentage of distributable profit that will be IBB's share of profit, for a calculation period, is shown in Table 10.2.

Table 10.2 Percentage of distributable profit

Savings accounts	IBB's share of distributable profit as at 2008* (%)
Undetermined term: 'savings account'	50
Young persons savings account	50
Direct savings account	40
Term deposit accounts	
One month – minimum 30 days, less than 90 days	45
Three months – minimum 90 days, less than 180 days	42.5
Six months – minimum 180 days	40

*These percentages are maximum figures and the Islamic Bank of Britain may reduce its share of profit, operating fees and expenses, and the profit stabilisation reserve contribution at its discretion.

10.3.4.4   *IBB* halal *Personal Finance Facility*

IBB's *halal* personal finance facility is an unsecured cash generating facility that allows customers to generate cash for the purpose of purchasing goods or services, such as:

- buying a car;
- refinancing a conventional loan;
- holidays;
- home improvements;
- paying for a wedding.

The customer may apply for a *halal* personal finance facility for a minimum of £5000 up to a maximum of £25,000 and has a choice of repayment periods.

There are two rates available for unsecured personal finance – one for home owners and one for non-home owners. IBB are the first fully *Sharia'a*-compliant bank to offer this facility in the UK. Finance is not secured, it is still unsecured, but IBB is able to offer preferential rates to home owners.

Like all IBB accounts, this *halal* facility has been approved by the IBB's *Sharia'a* Supervisory Board. The *halal* personal finance facility is based on the Islamic principle of *Murabaha*. IBB buys and sells commodities and generates profit from these transactions. It does not charge interest, and the customers do not pay interest to IBB.

How does IBB Generate Cash for the halal *Personal Finance Facility?*

The process of generating cash for the customer, through the IBB *halal* personal finance facility, would be as follows for a home owner facility of £10,000 over 12 months. Typical cost is 8.9% APR, as at 2008. The reason for quoting an APR is so that customers can make comparisons. The steps are as follows:

1. Customer requires £10,000 for 12 months.
2. Customer enters into agreement to buy a commodity from IBB on an agreed deferred payment period of 12 months.
3. IBB sells the commodity to the customer at cost plus profit to be paid over the agreed period of time.
4. Once in possession of the title to the commodity, the customer appoints a third party broker to sell the commodity on his behalf.
5. The proceeds from the sale of the commodity are credited to the customer's account. The quantity of the commodity used in this transaction would enable the customer to generate the cash required.
6. Customer has available funds of £10,000.
7. Customer makes monthly repayments.

Power of Attorney

As the customer is not present during the commodity transaction, he gives an IBB employee a restricted Power of Attorney to agree to purchase the commodity on his behalf.

The customer also signs an agency agreement appointing a broker to sell the commodity on his behalf.

In relation to the commodity transactions, both the purchase and sale are carried out on the same day to minimise the risk of price movement.

Membership of the Financial Services Compensation Scheme

The Islamic Bank of Britain PLC is a member of the Financial Services Compensation Scheme. The scheme may provide compensation if IBB cannot meet its obligations. For example, in respect of deposits with a UK office, payments under the scheme are limited to 100% of the first £2000 of a depositor's total deposits with the bank and 90% of the next £33,000, resulting in a maximum payment of £31,700.These guarantees are subject to change. Most depositors, including individuals and small firms are covered. The scheme covers deposits made with the offices of IBB within the European Economic Area.

10.3.4.5   Halal *Home Finance*

IBB has teamed up with the Arab Banking Corporation International Bank (ABCIB) to introduce customers to Alburaq Home Finance.

This relationship has been approved by the IBB *Sharia'a* Supervisory Board, who are satisfied that the technical resources complement IBB's expertise in bringing *halal* financial products and services to the marketplace.

How Does It Work?

Sharia'a-compliant home finance is based on the accepted and widely used Islamic financing principles of *Ijara* (leasing) and *Musharaka* (partnership). For example, a bank may contribute 90% and the customer 10% of the purchase price. Over a period of up to 25 years, the customer makes monthly purchase instalments through which the bank sells its share (90%) of the home to the customer. With each instalment paid, the bank's share in the property diminishes while the customer's share correspondingly increases.

10.3.5   How does IBB Ensure that its Products are *Sharia'a* Compliant?

The IBB's *Sharia'a* Supervisory Board has sole responsibility when deciding on matters relating to *Sharia'a* compliancy. It is comprised of world-renowned scholars, representing a wide spectrum of the Islamic faith, who are expert in the interpretation of Islamic law and its application within modern-day Islamic financial institutions. They ensure that *Sharia'a* compliance is at the heart of everything IBB does and every product and service that it offers.

10.3.5.1   *The* Sharia'a *Supervisory Board's Role*

The SSB meets on a regular basis to review all contracts and agreements relating to IBB's transactions as well as to advise it, guide it and sanction any new services that it introduces.

The SSB certifies every account and service that IBB provides. Without the SSB's approval, IBB cannot introduce a new product or service.

10.3.5.2   The Members of the IBB Sharia'a Supervisory Board

Sheikh Dr Abdul Sattar Abu Ghuddah (Chairman)

Sheikh Dr Abdul Sattar Abu Ghuddah is one of the world's leading scholars in the field of Islamic finance. He holds a PhD in Islamic Law from Al Azhar University, Cairo, Egypt.

Dr Abdul Sattar has taught at various institutes, including the Imam Al Da'awa Institute in Riyadh, the Religious Institute in Kuwait and the *Sharia'a* College and Law faculty at Kuwait University. He is the Secretary General of the Unified *Sharia'a* Supervisory Board of Dallah Albaraka Group in Jeddah, a member of the Islamic Fiqh Council in Jeddah and a member of the AAOIFI *Sharia'a* Board.

Sheikh Nizam Muhammed Seleh Yaqoobi

Sheikh Nizam is a member of a number of *Sharia'a* Supervisory Boards including the Dow Jones Islamic Index, Bahrain Islamic Bank and the Citi Islamic Investment Bank. He is also a member of the AAOIFI *Sharia'a* Board and has been a visiting lecturer at Harvard University.

Mufti Abdul Qadir Barkatulla

Mufti Barkatulla is a prominent *Sharia'a* scholar with a strong background in economics and finance. He is a member of the *Sharia'a* Supervisory Boards of several Islamic financial institutions including United National Bank, Alburaq of Arab Banking Corporation London and Lloyds TSB. He is also a senior Imam of Finchley Masjid in London, UK.

Sheikh Muhammad Taqi Usmani (Previous Member)

Sheikh Muhammad Taqi Usmani was a member of the *Sharia'a* Cassation Board at the Supreme Court in Pakistan from 1982 to 2002. He has been Vice President of Dar Al Uloom University, Karachi since 1974; Chairman of Islamic Economy Centre in Pakistan; Chairman of the *Sharia'a* Board of AAOIFI and sits on a number of *Sharia'a* boards of other institutions.

10.3.5.3   Sharia'a *Approval – Certificates of Endorsement* (Fatawa)

All IBB products and services have the approval of the *Sharia'a* Supervisory Board. Once approved, *Fatawa* are issued. The following *Fatawa* have been issued:

- Current Account certificate;
- Treasury Deposit Account certificate;
- Master *Murabaha* certificate;
- Commercial Property Finance certificate;
- Personal Finance certificate;
- Savings and Term Deposit certificate;
- Secured Business Finance certificate;
- Unsecured Business Finance certificate;
- Young Persons Savings certificate;
- Direct Savings Account certificate.

10.3.6   Financial Statements for 2005 and 2006

Table 10.3   Income statement for the year ended 31 December 2006

	2006 £	2005 £
Income receivable from:		
Islamic financing transactions	4,554,578	2,985,143
Returns payable to customers and banks	(1,705,389)	(814,978)
Net income from Islamic financing transactions	2,849,189	2,170,165
Fee and commission income	174,554	40,963
Fee and commission expense	(12,764)	(3167)
Net fee and commission income	161,790	37,796
Operating income	3,010,979	2,207,961
Net impairment loss on financial assets	(445,089)	(52,068)
Personnel expenses	(4,241,778)	(3,250,576)
General and administrative expenses	(5,430,902)	(3,859,216)
Depreciation	(621,462)	(754,689)
Amortisation	(1,105,001)	(740,919)
Total operating expenses	(11,844,232)	(8,657,468)
Loss before income tax	(8,833,253)	(6,449,507)
Income tax expense	–	–
Loss for the year	(8,833,253)	(6,449,507)
Loss per ordinary share (basic and diluted) – pence	(2.1)	(1.5)

Table 10.4   Balance sheet as at 31 December 2006

	2006 £	2005 £
Assets		
Cash	451,492	579,251
Commodity *Murabaha* and *Wakala* receivables and other advances to banks	100,286,964	78,037,676
Consumer finance accounts and other advances to customers	8,092,326	4,454,369
Net investment in commercial property finance	2,338,401	–
Property and equipment	3,965,370	3,798,951
Intangible assets	1,894,272	1,509,005
Other assets	983,270	910,248
Total assets	118,012,095	89,289,500
Liabilities and equity		
Liabilities		
Deposits from banks	240,164	
Deposits from customers	83,853,383	47,714,593
Other liabilities	2,187,261	1,010,367
Total liabilities	86,280,808	48,724,960
Equity		
Called up share capital	4,190,000	4,190,000
Share premium	48,747,255	48,747,255
Retained deficit	(21,205,968)	(12,372,715)
Total equity	31,731,287	40,564,540
Total equity and liabilities	118,012,095	89,289,500

10.4 CASE STUDY QUESTIONS

1. Outline the key issues that the FSA takes into account when granting a banking licence.

2. What issues did the FSA highlight as being particularly different with Islamic banks?

3. How was the issue of the definition of 'deposits' addressed by the FSA?

4. What role does the *Sharia'a* Supervisory Board play at IBB in contrast with that of the role played by the conventional board of directors?

5. Summarise the difference between the products offered by IBB and those of a conventional bank.

6. Regarding the financial shape of IBB, what conclusion would you draw from the income statement and balance sheet (see Tables 10.3 and 10.4)?

Case Study 11: Leverage and Islamic Banking

11.1 LEARNING OUTCOMES

After working through Case Study 11 you should be able to do the following:

- Define leverage.
- Explain why leverage is important within banking.
- Identify those items on a balance sheet that have leverage implications.
- Describe why Islamic banks do not favour conventional leverage.
- Contrast conventional leverage with Islamic leverage.
- Identify the issues raised by not having leverage.
- Explain the advantages and disadvantages of leverage.
- Define EBIT.
- Explain how EBIT is affected by leverage.
- Define EBT.
- Explain how EBT is affected by leverage.
- Define EAT.
- Explain how EAT is affected by leverage.
- Define ROE.
- Explain how ROE is affected by leverage.
- Define EPS.
- Explain how EPS is affected by leverage.
- Identify the downside for Islamic banks of not having leverage.
- Describe the upside for Islamic banks of not having leverage.

11.2 LEVERAGE AND ISLAMIC BANKING

Case Abstract

Conventional banks use leverage – the use of debt in their balance sheets – as a powerful tool to magnify returns. The cost of this debt is the interest that has to be paid to finance it. The prohibition of interest for Islamic banks severely constrains the magnification benefits available to them. Replicating the gains from leverage for Islamic banks becomes much more difficult. This case study highlights the potential costs of the *riba* prohibition for an Islamic bank, in terms of the impact on EBIT, EAT, EBT, ROE and EPS. Needless to say there can also be financial benefits from not having leverage!

11.3   WHAT IS FINANCIAL LEVERAGE?

Financial leverage takes the form of borrowing (debt), the proceeds of which are reinvested with the objective being to earn a higher rate of return than the interest cost. If the bank's return on assets (ROA) is higher than the interest on the loan, its return on equity (ROE) will be higher than if it did not borrow. On the other hand if the bank's ROA is lower than the interest rate, its ROE will be lower than if it did not borrow.

Leverage allows greater potential returns to the investor than otherwise would have been available. The potential for loss is also greater, however, because if the investment severely under performs the borrowings and all accrued interest payments on the borrowings still need to be repaid to the lenders.

Traditionally, Islamic banks do not have interest-related debt, thereby changing the potential impact of leverage on their financial ratios. There are a variety of ways for conventional banks to achieve financial leverage, discussed in this case. They are based on some form of debt to equity ratio.

11.3.1   What is the Debt to Equity Ratio?

Debt to equity is generally measured as the bank's total liabilities (excluding shareholders' equity) divided by shareholders' equity:

$$D/E = \text{Debt to equity ratio}$$
$$D/(D + E) = \text{Debt to value ratio}$$

where D = liabilities, E = equity and A = total assets.

11.4   FINANCIAL TERMINOLOGY: A GUIDE

11.4.1   Earnings Before Interest and Taxes (EBIT)

In financial and business accounting, EBIT is a measure of a bank's profitability that excludes interest and income tax expenses:

$$EBIT = \text{Operating Revenue} - \text{Operating Expenses} + \text{Nonoperating Income}$$
$$\text{Operating Income} = \text{Operating Revenue} - \text{Operating Expenses}$$

'Operating income' is the difference between operating revenues and operating expenses, but it is also sometimes used as a synonym for EBIT and operating profit. This is true if the bank has no nonoperating income.

To calculate EBIT, expenses (e. g., the cost of banking services provided, selling and administrative expenses) are subtracted from revenues. Profit is later obtained by subtracting interest and taxes from the result (see Box 11.1).

11.4.1.1   How do You Interpret EBIT?

EBIT is an indicator of bank's profitability, calculated as revenue minus expenses, excluding tax and interest. EBIT is also referred to as 'operating earnings', 'operating profit' and 'operating income', because one can rearrange the formula to be calculated as follows:

$$EBIT = \text{Revenue} - \text{Operating Expenses}$$

Box 11.1 Income statement – example for a conventional bank (figures in US$ millions)

Operating revenues	
Net income	**20,438**
Operating expenses	
Cost of providing banking facilities	7943
Selling, general and administrative expenses	8172
Depreciation	960
Other expenses	138
Total operating expenses	**17,213**
Operating income	3225
Nonoperating income	130
Earnings before interest and income taxes (EBIT)	**3355**
Net interest expense	145
Earnings before income taxes	3210
Income taxes	1027
Net income	**2183**

In other words, EBIT is all profits before taking into account interest payments and income taxes.

An important factor contributing to the widespread use of EBIT is the way in which it neutralises the effects of the different capital structures and tax rates used by different banks.

By excluding both taxes and interest expenses, the figure hones in on the bank's ability to make profits.

11.4.2   Earnings before tax (EBT)

EBT is an indicator of a bank's financial performance and is calculated as

$$EBT = Revenue - Expenses\ (excluding\ tax)$$

EBT provides a level measure to compare banks in different tax jurisdictions or where there are no taxes at all.

11.4.3   Earnings after tax (EAT)

EAT provides a level measure to compare financial banks performance after tax.

11.4.4   Return on equity (ROE)

ROE measures the rate of return on the ownership interest (shareholders' equity) of the common stock owners. ROE is viewed as one of the most important financial ratios.

ROE measures a bank's efficiency at generating profits from every dollar of net assets (assets minus liabilities), and shows how well a bank uses investment dollars to generate earnings growth. ROE is equal to a fiscal year's net income (after preferred stock dividends but before common stock dividends) divided by total equity (excluding preferred shares), expressed as a percentage:

$$ROE = \frac{\text{Net income}}{\text{Average stockholders' equity}}$$

11.4.5   Earnings per share (EPS)

EPS measures the portion of a bank's profit allocated to each outstanding share of common stock. EPS serves as an indicator of a bank's profitability.

EPS is calculated as

$$EPS = \frac{\text{Net Income}}{\text{Average Outstanding Shares}}$$

Earnings per share is generally considered to be the single most important variable in determining the share price. It is also a major component of the price-to-earnings valuation ratio.

11.5   CASE STUDY ASSUMPTIONS

The case study assumptions are given in Table 11.1.

Table 11.1   XYZ Conventional Bank

	($ millions)								
Debt ratio (%)	10	20	30	40	50	60	70	80	90
Capital									
(1000) Debt	100	200	300	400	500	600	700	800	900
Equity	900	800	700	600	500	400	300	200	100
Total	1000	1000	1000	1000	1000	1000	1000	1000	1000
Shares @ $10	90K	80K	70K	60K	50K	40K	30K	20K	10K0
Revenue	1000	1000	1000	1000	1000	1000	1000	1000	1000
Cost/expense	800	800	800	800	800	800	800	800	800
EBIT									
Interest									
EBT									
Tax									
EAT									
ROE									
EPS									
Interest rate	10%								
Tax rate	40%								

11.6   CASE STUDY QUESTIONS

The questions are based on Table 11.1.

1. For a bank with debt, calculate and comment on the effect of changing levels of debt on

    1.1   EBIT

     ✎ _____

     _____

     _____

     _____

    1.2   EBT

     ✎ _____

     _____

     _____

     _____

    1.3   EAT

     ✎ _____

     _____

     _____

     _____

    1.4   ROE. See also Question 2.

     ✎ _____

     _____

     _____

     _____

    1.5   EPS

     ✎ _____

     _____

     _____

     _____

2. Plot graphically the relationship between changing leverage and ROE.
3. For a bank with no conventional debt (an Islamic bank), calculate and comment on the effect of changing levels of debt on the following (use the same assumptions as for the conventional bank above):

3.1 EBIT

_____

_____

_____

_____

3.2 EBT

_____

_____

_____

_____

3.3 EAT

_____

_____

_____

_____

3.4 ROE

_____

_____

_____

_____

3.5 EPS

_____

_____

_____

_____

4. Highlight the key differences between the conventional and Islamic banks regarding the effect of leverage on their financial ratios.

_____

_____

_____

_____

12

Case Study 12: Impact of Non-performing Loans on Islamic and Conventional Banks

12.1 LEARNING OUTCOMES

After working through Case Study 12 you should be able to do the following:

- Define non-performing loans.
- Explain why non-performing loans are important for conventional banks.
- Illustrate why non-performing loans are important for Islamic banks.
- Explain why non-performing loans should not be an issue for the shareholders of Islamic banks.
- Describe the strategies applied by Islamic banks to minimise the effect of non-performing loans.
- Distinguish equity-based versus debt-based banking.
- Describe the risk sharing principles applied by Islamic banks.
- Identify the extra risks for Islamic banks of applying risk sharing principles.
- Define the different implications for Islamic banks compared with conventional banks with regards to non-performing loans.

12.2 ISLAMIC BANKING PRINCIPLES INVOLVE RISK SHARING, WHICH SHOULD MAKE THEM LESS VULNERABLE THAN THEIR CONVENTIONAL COUNTERPARTS

Case Abstract

The crux of the Islamic economic system is the sharing of profits and losses. The vast majority of liabilities and assets in the balance sheet of an Islamic bank are risk capital. In good times the depositors and the shareholders share the profits and in bad times they share the losses. In the conventional banking system the value of deposits is guaranteed by the bank, plus there is a guarantee of the payment of interest. Any economic shock or a business downturn adversely affects the quality and value of the assets of a conventional bank leading, potentially, to the balance sheet of the bank moving towards negative net worth. This outcome is not necessarily the case for an Islamic bank. Exposure to non-performing loans affects Islamic and conventional banks in different ways. This case study examines those differences.

12.3 EQUITY-BASED VERSUS DEBT-BASED BANKING

The operations of Islamic financial institutions, particularly on the liability side of the balance sheet, are primarily based on a profit and loss sharing (PLS) principle. An Islamic bank does not charge interest but rather participates in the yield resulting from the use of funds. The depositors also share in the profits of the bank according to a predetermined ratio. There is thus a partnership between the Islamic bank and its depositors, on the asset side, and between the bank and its investment clients, on the liability side, as a manager of depositors' resources in productive uses.

This is in contrast with a conventional bank, which mainly borrows funds paying interest on one side of the balance sheet and lends funds charging interest on the other. The complexity of Islamic banking comes from the variety (and nomenclature) of the instruments employed, and in understanding the underpinnings of *Sharia'a* law.

An Islamic bank operates on an equity-based system, unlike the debt-based conventional banking system. In a pure Islamic financial system, shocks to the assets position of a bank are immediately absorbed by investors and shareholders in proportion to their share.

Apart from its own funds (Capital + Reserves + Retained Profits), an Islamic bank relies for its source of funds mainly on investment deposits, which are also termed as profit and loss accounts and, more often, Restricted and Unrestricted investment deposits. These are the principal sources of funds for Islamic banks. In both intent and content these are much nearer to shareholdings (equities) in the bank rather than the fixed or saving deposits of a conventional bank. An Islamic bank's deposits are not formally guaranteed, unlike conventional bank deposits.

The terms and conditions of the deposits received by Islamic banks make clear, to the investors concerned, their participation in both the potential profit and potential loss, if any. This information enables the investors to take a calculated decision as far as the risks are involved, when making their investment with an Islamic bank.

The difference between a conventional share (equity) and an Islamic investment deposit is that the share capital is permanent and cannot be moved, whereas Islamic investment deposits are term investments.

In order to maintain liquidity at all times, thereby ensuring the availability of funds for financing and to avoid any potential mismatch, the Treasurer of an Islamic bank matches the maturities of the investors' funds with the investments and financing. A prudent ratio of availability of investors' funds helps in projecting and preparing a business plan for mobilisation of the funds, so as to be able to meet the liquidity requirements at all times.

The conventional banking liquidity management system is based on short-term borrowing for pre-agreed, guaranteed, fixed returns to depositors.

Islamic banks distribute profits evenly taking the cue from the Islamic injunction of mutual cooperation and liability. To quote the *Qur'an*:

> Cooperate with one another in righteousness and piety, and do not cooperate in sin and transgression.
>
> *Qur'an 5: 2*

12.4 CASE STUDY ASSUMPTIONS

Within the economy assume that there is a conventional and an Islamic bank as follows:

- Both banks are located in the same country, the same banking market and under the control of the same Central Bank.

- Working capital is 50 million for both banks.
- The capital/deposit ratio is 15:1 for both banks.
- Both banks make a profit of 11%.
- The conventional bank pays 10% interest to its depositors.
- The Islamic bank pays nothing to its depositors until the net profit of the bank becomes clear at the end of the year. At that stage the net profit is distributed among the depositors' investment accounts.
- Both banks suffer negatively as a result of losses and bankruptcies with non-performing loans of 40 million.

12.5   CASE STUDY QUESTIONS

1. What is the initial balance sheet/profit and loss statement for each bank, after being fully capitalised?

   _____

   _____

   _____

   _____

2. How do the profits made, and interest paid, change the income statement for each bank?

   _____

   _____

   _____

   _____

3. How do the income statements compare after allowing for non-performing loans?

   _____

   _____

   _____

   _____

4. Assuming that the Islamic bank pays out all its profits, what is the payout to its depositors?

   _____

   _____

   _____

   _____

5. What are the prospects for both banks after adjustments of the financial statements for the non-performing loans?

   _____

   _____

   _____

   _____

Case Study Answers

CASE STUDY 1: *IJARA* CONTRACT

Case Answers

1–5: Answers can be found in the case study text itself.
6. 6,683.1
7. 10,474.4
8. 8,108
9. 7,471.1
10. 9,597.6
11. 8,290.4
12. Several features of the scheme are, in fact, very similar to *Ijara Wa-Iktina.*

CASE STUDY 2: *MUSHARAKA* CONTRACT

Case 1 Answers

Answers to Questions 1 and 2 for all four projects are shown below.

Project 1: Mobile phone shop

Duration of *Musharaka*	One week
Bank's contribution	75%
Partner's contribution	25%
Bank's share in management	0%
Partner's share in management	30%
Bank's share in total profit	52.50%
Partner's share in total profit	47.50%

To start, the shares in total profit are calculated, and then the periodic, monthly and annual returns to the bank and partner are derived. The shares in the total profit depend upon two elements: (i) the contribution and (ii) the share in management.

Here the bank and partner have agreed to set aside 25% of the total profit for management and this will all go to the partner. The bank's and partner's contributions are 75% and 25%, respectively.

Imagine the firm makes £1000 profit. Of this £300 would go for management and would all accrue to the partner. Of the remaining £700, the bank would receive 75%, or £525, and the partner would receive £175. So the total receipts for the bank and partner would be £525 and £475 respectively. This would be a return of 52.5% and 47.5%.

The share in management is taken directly from the profit, and the share for the contribution of capital is a percentage of what is left over (i.e., a percentage of a percentage.)

Using these relationships, the shares in the profit may be derived. Notice that here the duration or the volume of the *Musharaka* are not relevant. The percentage of the profit that will be received is the same, no matter what the period or size of investment.

Project 2: Flower Nursery

Duration of *Musharaka*	One week
Bank's contribution	50%
Partner's contribution	50%
Bank's share in management	0%
Partner's share in management	60%
Bank's share in total profit	20%
Partner's share in total profit	80%

The total returns need to be calculated first. The volume of *Musharaka* (£200,000) and the *total* monthly return (50%) are given. As the project lasts for one week, the weekly (periodic) return will be one quarter of 50% or 12.5%.

If the periodic return is 12.5% and the volume of *Musharaka* is £200,000, it follows that the profit/income is £25,000. This is distributed according to the shares in total profit in the above table. The bank will receive 20% (or £5000) of this and 80% (or £20,000) will go to the partner. As the bank contributed 50% of the *Musharaka*, or £100,000, the *periodic* return to the bank will be £5000 as a percentage of the contribution of £100,000 (or 5%). The partner's contribution is worked out in a similar way: the partner receives £20,000 on an investment of £100,000, or a *periodic* return of 20%.

Multiplying these returns by four gives the 20% and 80% figures for the monthly rates and multiplying again by 12 gives the 240% and 960% annual returns, as shown below.

Shares in profit	One week
Bank	20%
Partner	80%
Total	100%

Shares in profit	One week
Periodic rates of return	
Bank	5%
Partner	20%
Total	12.5%
Monthly rates of return	
Bank	20%
Partner	80%
Total	50%
Annual rates of return	
Bank	240%
Partner	960%
Total	600%

Project 3: Coffee Shop

Duration of *Musharaka*	Four months
Bank's contribution	50%
Partner's contribution	50%
Bank's share in management	1.20%
Partner's share in management	87.70%
Bank's share in total profit	6.75%
Partner's share in total profit	93.25%

The volume of *Musharaka* is £1,000,000 and the total four-monthly return is 45% (note that the period is not one but four months). This gives £450,000 for four months. Of this, the bank receives 6.75% or 30,375 and the partner receives £419,625.

As their contributions are both 50%, or £500,000, the *periodic* (in this case quarterly) returns will be 30,375/500,000 or 6.075% for the bank and 419,625/500,000 or 83.925% for the partner. These answers are to be found (rounded) in the following table under the heading 'monthly returns'. Dividing these by four gives the true monthly returns or 1.15875% and 20.98125% respectively. Simply multiply these by 12 to get the annual returns.

Here 88.9% of the total profits have been allocated for the share in management and the remaining 11.1% for the contributions. If the firm makes £1000 profit, £889 will be allocated according to the agreed shares in management. So the bank will receive £12 and the partner £877. This leaves £111 to be distributed according to the contributions. So, in this case the amount is split 50:50, with each party receiving £55.50.

In total, therefore, the bank receives £67.50, a return of 6.75%, and the partner receives £932.50, a return of 93.25%, as shown in Figure A2.1.

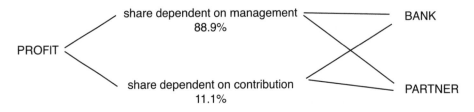

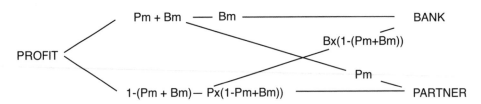

Figure A2.1   Coffee shop returns

Shares in profit	Four months
Bank	6.75%
Partner	93.25%
Total	100%
Periodic rates of return	
Bank	6.075%
Partner	83.925%
Total	45%
Monthly rates of return	
Bank	1.15875%
Partner	20.98125%
Total	11.25%
Annual rates of return	
Bank	18.225%
Partner	251.775%
Total	135%

Project 4: Internet cafe

This follows the same principle as the previous three projects.

Summary of Case 1 Answers

Description	Mobile phone shop	Flower nursery	Coffee shop	Internet cafe
Duration of *Musharaka*	One week	One week	Four months	One month
Duration in week (D)	1	1	16	4
Bank contribution B	75%	50%	50%	14%
Partner's contribution P	25%	50%	50%	86%
Bank's share in management P_M	0%	0%	1.20%	5%
Partner's share in management B_M	30%	60%	87.70%	25%
Shares in profit				
Bank B_T	52.5%	20%	6.75%	14.8%
Partner P_T	47.5%	80%	93.25%	85.2%
Total	100%	100%	100%	100%
Volume of *Musharaka* (V)	29,295	200,000	1,000,000	1,000,000
Implied profit for a month (I)	65,503	100,000	112,500	66,000
Profit over the duration of *Musharaka*	16,375.905	25,000	450,000	66,000
Periodic rates of return				
Bank	39.13%	5%	6.075%	6.977%
Partner	106.2%	20%	83.925%	6.537%
Total	55.9%	12.5%	45%	6.6%
Monthly rates of return				
Bank	122%	20%	6%	5.2%
Partner	325.3%	80%	84%	6.8%
Total	223.60%	50%	45%	6.60%
Annual rates of return				
Bank	1464%	240%	18.225%	62.4%
Partner	3904%	960%	251.775%	81.6%
Total	2803%	600%	135%	78.9%

Case 2 Answers

A Sudanese Islamic bank invested into a grocery store for a one month period, employing a *Musharaka* contract. The investment contributions of the bank and the grocery store partner with the net profit are given in the following table (£ Sudanese).

	Bank	Partner	Total
Investment	735	690	1425
Percentage	52%	48%	100%
Net profit	179	271	450

It was agreed that the profit distribution for the management of the project should be 37% for the bank and 63% for the grocery store. The 37% was to be distributed as being 30% of the partner's percentage in the management with the bank contributing 7% of the management.

It was also agreed that the 63% would be divided up as being 30% of the partner's percentage of the profit and 33% as being the bank's percentage of the profit.

Here the income is given as 450 in the question (see Table 2.2).

Answers to Questions 3 to 8 are shown in the following table.

	Partner	Bank	Total
Profit distribution (as per agreement)			
Question 3. 37% for management			166.5
30% partner's % in management		135	
7% bank's % in management	31.5		
Question 4. 63% for shared profit			283.5
30% partner's % in the profit		**135**	
33% banks in the profit	**148.5**		
Total profits	**180**	**270**	**450**
Rate of return on investment			
Question 5. Partner's rate on return/monthly	26.09%		
Question 6. Partner's rate of return/annually	**313%**		
Question 7. Bank's rate of return/monthly		**39.13%**	
Question 8. Bank's rate of return/annually		**469.57%**	

CASE STUDY 3: DIMINISHING *MUSHARAKA* CONTRACT

Case Answers

1. Based on the rental value and the financing period, determine the monthly repayment schedule that results in the client fully owning the property at the end of the agreed rental term. Answers are shown in the following table.

Up to the end of	Bank		Customer		Units purchased at the end of the year
	Units	Rental/month	Units	Rental/month	
Year 1	8	60,000	2	15,000	2
Year 2	6	45,000	4	30,000	2
Year 3	4	30,000	6	45,000	2
Year 4	2	15,000	8	60,000	2
Year 5	0	0	10	Customer is the owner at this point	

2. No specific answer is given here because the information is clearly provided in the chapter text.

CASE STUDY 4: *MUDARABA* CONTRACT

Case 1 Answers

Answers to Questions 1 and 2 are contained in the following completed table and explanatory text.

	(1) Average funds available for invest- ments	(2) Investment rate	(3) Weighted average of invested funds (1 × 2)	(4) Percentage of weighted average of invested funds	(5) Net profit from investments (millions)	(6) Shareholders' share of net profit before the *Mudarib* share (4 × 5)	(7) Shareholders' share of the *Mudarib*'s profit*	(8) Distributable profit after shareholders' share of the *Mudarib*'s profit (6 – 7) (millions)	(9) Rate of return (8/1)
Shareholders	130	100%	130	130/1,045 = 12.44%	75	9.33	–	24.99**	19.22%
Investment accounts: One year	150	90%	135	135/1,045 = 12.92%	75	9.69	1.45	8.24	5.49%
Investment accounts: six months	450	80%	360	360/1,045 = 34.45%	75	25.84	5.17	20.67	4.59%
Investment savings accounts	700	60%	420	420/1,045 = 40.19%	75	30.14	9.04	21.10	3.01%
Total funds available for in- vestment	1,430		1,045						

* Column six multiplied by shareholders' ratio of profit allocation.
** Residual accruing to shareholders after payment to investment account holders.

Mudarada Contract with Various Partners

Profits: *Mudarib* is not entitled to any salary or commission other than his profit share
What does this mean?
Client receives 50% of profits from his capital contribution.
Client receives 50% of the total capital contribution of profit.
Bank receives 50% of capital contribution.
Residual from entrepreneur (that is, any income after the *Mudarib* share) is paid to the partner (the *Rab ul Mall*) in *Mudaraba*.
Losses: These are charged against the percentage of capital contributed only.

Case 2 Answers

Answers to Questions 3 and 4 are contained in the following table.

Assumptions	Capital contribution	Capital owner: exposed to loss
Mudarib	0	
Bank	100	X
Partner	0	
Third party *Mudarib*	0	
PLS	50/50	
Case 2 Calculations	Profits	Losses
1. Return to *Mudarib*		
Size of profits	10	−10
Total profits due	5	
Mudarib's capital contributions	0	
Mudarib's capital share (%)	0	
Total capital share of profits due	0	
Profit share + Capital share	5	
2. Return to bank		
Banks profit share	5	
Bank capital contribution	100	
Bank capital share (%)	100	
3. Total capital returned	100	
Mudarib	0	0
Bank	100	90
4. Total return (Capital returned +/− Profits/Losses)		
4.1 Profits		
Mudarib	5	
Bank	105	
4.2 Losses		
Mudarib	0	
Bank	90	

Case 3 Answers

Answers to Questions 5 and 6 are contained in the following table.

Assumptions	Capital contribution	Capital owner: exposed to loss
Mudarib	100	X
Bank	100	X
Partner	0	
Third party Mudarib	0	
PLS	50/50	
Case 3 Calculations	Profits	Losses
1. Return to Mudarib		
Size of profits	20	−20
Profit share	10	
Mudarib capital contributions	100	
Mudarib capital share (%)	50%	
Total capital share of profits due	5	
Total capital contributions	200	
Profit share + Capital share	15	
2. Return to banks		
Profit share	5	
Bank capital contribution	100	
Bank capital share (%)	50	
3. Capital returned	200	180
Bank	100	90
Mudarib	100	90
4. Total return (Capital returned + Profits/Losses)		
4.1 Profits		
Mudarib	115	
Bank	105	
4.2 Losses		
Mudarib	90	
Bank	90	

Case 4 Answers

Answers to Questions 7 and 8 are contained in the following table.

Assumptions	Capital contribution	Capital owner: exposed to loss
Mudarib	100 (bank loan)	X (responsible for loss)
Bank	100	X
Partner	0	
Third party Mudarib	0	
PLS	50/50	
Case 4 Calculations	Profits	Losses
1. Return to Mudarib		
Size of profits	20	−20
Profit share	10	
Mudarib capital contributions (bank loan)	100	
Mudarib capital share (%)	50%	
Total capital share of profits due	5	
Total capital contributions	200	
Profit share + Capital share	15	
2. Return to banks		
Bank capital contribution	100	
Bank capital share (%)	50	
Profit share	5	
3. Capital returned	200	180
Bank (own capital)	100	90
Bank (bank loan)	100	100
Mudarib	100	
Owes bank		100
Owed from capital share		90
Net loss to *Mudarib*		−10

4. Total return (Capital returned + Profits/Losses)

4.1 Profits

Mudarib	15	
Bank (including return of bank loan)	205	

4.2 Losses

Mudarib	90	
Bank (including return of bank loan)	180	

Case 5 Answers

Answers to Questions 9 and 10 are contained in the following table.

Assumptions	Capital contribution	Capital owner: exposed to loss
Mudarib	100	X
Bank	100	X
Partner	0	
Third party *Mudarib*	100	X
PLS	33/33/33	
Mudarib/third party		
Mudaraba 50/50 PLS		
Case 5 Calculations	Profits	Losses
Size of profits	30	−30
1. Return to Mudarib		
Total profits due	10	
Mudarib capital contributions	100	
Mudarib capital share (%)	33%	
Total capital share of profits due	10	
Profit share + Capital share	20	
2. Return to third party Mudaraba		
(50% of profits made by *Mudarib*)	5	
Third party *Mudaraba* capital contribution	100	
Mudarib capital share	33%	
3. Return to bank		
Bank residual (50% of Profits left)	5	
Bank capital contribution	100	
Bank capital share (%)	33	
4. Capital returned		
Bank	100	90
Mudarib	100	90
Third party *Mudaraba*	100	90
5. Total return (Capital returned +/− Profits/Losses)		
5.1 Profits		
Mudarib	120	
Bank	105	
Third party *Mudaraba*	105	
5.2 Losses		
Mudarib	90	
Bank	90	
Third party *Mudaraba*	90	

Case 6 Answers

Answers to Questions 11 and 12 are contained in the following table.

Assumptions	Capital contribution	Capital owner: exposed to loss
Mudarib	0	
Bank	100	X
Business partner	100	X
PLS *Mudarib*/partner 50/50		
PLS *Mudarib*/bank 50/50		
Case 6 Calculations	Profits	Losses
Size of profits	20	20
1. Return to *Mudarib*		
Agreed profit share (%)		
1. With partner	50/50	
2. With bank	50% of entrepreneur's profit	
Total profits due	5	
Mudarib capital contributions	0	
Mudarib capital share (%)	0	
Total capital share of profits due	0	
Profit share + Capital share	5	
2. Return to partner		
Partner's profit share	10	
Partner's capital contribution	100	
Partner's capital share (%)	50	
3. Return to bank: residual		
Banks profit share	5	
Bank capital contribution	100	
Bank capital share (%)	50	
4. Capital returned		
Mudarib	0	0
Partner	100	90
Bank	100	90
5. Total return (Capital returned +/− Profits/Losses)		
5.1 Profits		
Mudarib	5	
Bank	105	
Partner	110	
5.2 Losses		
Mudarib	0	
Bank	90	
Partner	90	

CASE STUDY 5: *MURABAHA, MUDARABA, IJARA* AND *IJARA WA IQTINA*

Case 1 Answers

Answers to Questions 1 to 5 are contained in the following table.

	Conventional bank loan	*Murabaha*
Question 1. What are the key areas of concern?	Provider of funds is concerned primarily with customers credit-worthiness	Provider of funds is concerned about the goods sold and shares part of the risk of the transaction. The existence of a real, tangible, commodity is the rationale for this contract.
Question 2. How would you categorise the bank–customer relationship?	Borrower–Lender	Seller–Buyer
Question 3. Are the returns to the bank fixed or variable?	Fixed interest rate, but occasionally variable rate	Profit in terms of a margin over the cost of acquiring the sold commodity.
Question 4. Are there any guarantees?	Collateral is usually used against the loan	Collateral is usually used to ensure repayment.
Question 5. What happens if the borrower defaults?	Interest will be charged for any default period	Once concluded, a sale price cannot be changed. In some cases a penalty will be charged.

Case 2 Answers

Musharaka *with profits*

Answers to Questions 6 and 7 are contained in the following table.

Islamic bank $8,000,000 80%	Investor $2,000,000 20%
Agreed that investor is to be paid 10% management fee as percentage of profit after expenses ($200,000)	
Sale proceeds Less expenses	12,400,000 200,000
Funds available Funds invested	12,200,000 10,000,000

Profit	2,200,000
Management fee	220,000
Total profit on funds =	1,980,000
Bank receives 80% share =	1,584,000
Plus $8 million =	8,000,000
Total return to the bank	**9,584,000**
Investors receive 20% share =	396,000
Management Fee =	200,000
Plus $2 million capital =	2,000,000
Total return to the investor	**2,596,000**

Musharaka *with Losses*

Answers to Questions 8 and 9 are contained in the following table.

Sale proceeds	9,200,000
Less expenses	200,000
Capital loss	800,000
Total loss	1,000,000
No profits and so no management fees	
Net loss of 1,000,000 shared by bank and client in ratio of 80/20%	
Total capital returned to the bank	**7,200,000**
Total capital returned to the investor	**1,800,000**
Note under *Musharaka*, losses are shared between bank and investor	

Case 3 Answer

Answer to Question 10 is shown in the following table.

	Year 1 ($)	Year 2 ($)	Year 3($)
Bank finance	2000	2000	2000
Insurance	600	600	600
Profit required by bank	900	700	500
Yearly rental charge	3500	3300	3100
Quarterly rental charge	875	825	775
Book value after three years is $4000.			
Risk for lessor of default by the lessee			

Case 4 Answer

Answer to Question 11 is shown in the following table.

	Year 1 ($)	Year 2 ($)	Year 3($)
Bank finance	3330	3330	3330
Profit required by bank	900	700	500
Yearly rental charge	4230	4030	3830
Quarterly rental charge	1057	1007	957
Risk of loss is now with the lessee.			

Case 5 Answer

The answer to Question 12 is shown in the flow chart in Figure A5.1.

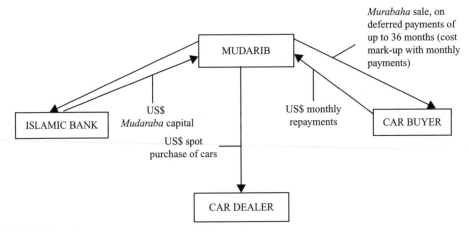

Figure A5.1   The role played by each party in the car *Mudaraba* with *Murabaha* transaction

CASE STUDY 6: ISLAMIC HOME FINANCE

Case Answers

1. What are the key principles underlying both conventional and Islamic home financing techniques?

   Conventional house finance: Bank lending, i.e., a bank provides a pure interest based loan. In this case, the bank extends a loan to a borrower to buy a house and charges interest. Repayment takes place over the life of the loan

   Islamic house finance – Murabaha: Sale and purchase, i.e., the bank buys the house first, and then sells it at an agreed profit. The sale can either be a bullet payment for cash or seller agrees to sell the property on an instalment basis factoring in a fixed profit over a certain period of time.

   Islamic Finance – Ijara wa Iqtina: The rental reflects capital redemption.

   Islamic Finance – Diminishing Musharaka: Mark-up priced in.

   Answers to Question 1 are summarised in the following table.

	Conventional home finance	Islamic home finance
Financing principle (1)	Bank loan	Sale and purchase (*Murabaha*)
Profit versus interest (2)	Interest charged	Mark-up priced in
Ownership (Title) (3)	Consumer has title	Financier has title

2. What is the role of profit versus interest in conventional and Islamic home financing transactions?

   Conventional house finance: Interest margin. Bank extends a loan at a premium, i.e., with an interest rate that varies according to the risk and the interest rate outlook.

   Islamic house finance: Profit margin. Both parties agree to a certain amount of profit arising from the sale and purchase. The profit should be earned in full even if full payment is settled prematurely.

3. Who retains the title to the property in each transaction?

   Conventional finance: In a conventional loan secured by a mortgage, the consumer has ownership but not title.

   Islamic house finance: In *Ijara* and Diminishing *Musharaka*, the title is with the financier. In *Murabaha*, it transfers to the consumer with a lien or mortgage granted.

4. What are the *Sharia'a* rules applied in the case of home finance?

   To be a *Sharia'a*-compliant loan, the following principles need to apply.

   The loan must be free from a requirement by the borrower to pay interest. This does not, however, mean that *Sharia'a* law prohibits the concept of borrowing – rather the reverse, provided that the loan stimulates productivity in the economy, rather than the making of more money from money.

   The loan needs to demonstrate that the risks are shared fairly between the parties. A predetermined return to the lender, regardless of whether the transaction makes a profit, is not *Sharia'a* compliant.

   The loan must provide assistance to society by helping in the production of trade services and most commodities. The production of certain commodities is strictly banned, such as pork or alcohol.

No part of the loan must have any factor of uncertainty. Loans relating to certain speculative deals are therefore not allowed.

There must be a single contract, i.e., no hybridisation is permitted. The majority of schools of Islamic jurisprudence do not allow the combining of more than one contract into a single contract. For instance, a contract of sale and lease may not be combined into a single contract.

The form and substance distinction is important. Although Islamic scholars are very concerned with the substance of a contract, their initial point of evaluation is the form. This has, in part, to do with the categorisation of commercial contracts in Islamic legal analysis. The convergence between form and substance is that a for-profit financial transaction must involve goods, not money. Hence, an instalment contract to sell homes is permissible, but one to sell money is not. Both have similar substance to a loan, but different forms. For the *Sharia'a*, the distinguishing substantial matter is the existence and sale of a non-monetary asset.

Late payment is another issue. The concept of penalty interest is forbidden in the *Sharia'a* because it is seen as being identical to the forbidden *riba*. However, Islamic scholars have permitted lenders and lessors to be able to charge a flat fee commensurate with their costs of collection. There may not be any compounding of the fee. It is assessable one time per instance of tardiness.

5. Outline the key characteristics of *Murabaha* as a technique for home finance.

Murabaha is a form of asset finance that involves the lender purchasing the asset, back to back with a sale of the asset, to the borrower, at an increased price. This increased price usually reflects the interest that would otherwise be payable.

6. What are the differences between *Murabaha* and *Ijara* as techniques for home finance?

There is a key point of difference between *Murabaha* and *Ijara*. In *Murabaha* the actual sale should take place after the client takes delivery from the supplier, and any previous agreement of *Murabaha* is not enough for effecting the actual sale. Therefore, after taking possession of the asset under the agency agreement, the agent is bound to give intimation to the institution and make an offer for the purchase from him. The sale takes place after the institution accepts the offer.

The procedure in leasing is different, and a little shorter. Here the parties need not effect the lease contract after taking delivery. If the institution, while appointing the client as its agent, has agreed to lease the asset with effect from the date of delivery, the lease will automatically start on that date without any additional procedure.

There are two reasons for this difference between *Murabaha* and *Ijara*. First, it is a necessary condition for a valid *Sharia'a* sale that it should be effected instantly. Thus, a sale attributed to a future date is invalid in the *Sharia'a*. But leasing can be attributed to a future date. Therefore any previous agreement is not sufficient in the case of *Murabaha*, whereas it is quite acceptable in the case of leasing.

Second, the basic principle of *Sharia'a* is that one cannot claim a profit or a fee for a property, the risk on which was never borne.

Applying this principle to *Murabaha*, the seller cannot claim a profit over a property that never remained under his risk for a moment. Therefore, if any previous agreement is held to be sufficient for effecting a sale between the client and the institution, the asset shall be transferred to the client simultaneously when he takes its possession, and the asset shall not come into the risk of the seller even for a moment. That is why the simultaneous transfer is not possible in *Murabaha*, and there needs to be a fresh offer and acceptance after the delivery.

In leasing, however, the asset remains under the risk and ownership of the lessor throughout the lease period, because the ownership has not been transferred. Therefore, if the lease period begins from the time when the client has taken delivery it does not violate the *Sharia'a* principle mentioned above.

7. Outline the key characteristics of *Ijara wa Iqtina* as a technique for home finance. How do the payment arrangements differ from a conventional mortgage?

In a conventional mortgage loan, the client signs a contract to buy a property and comes to the bank for a loan. At the closing the bank lends the client the money, which is then given to the seller of the property and the client then gets the property in exchange. The client then has to pay the loan back to the bank over the duration of the financing.

Devon Bank and *Ijara*

Devon Bank has kindly provided to the author an excellent illustration of how it applies the *Ijara* principle with home finance. As they stress, a payment consists of three components:

1. Principal (paying back the actual amount borrowed).
2. Interest (profit to the bank based on the client's use of the bank's money).
3. Escrow items (sums to protect the party's interests, such as insurance premiums, and real estate taxes).

Principal and interest are computed according to an amortisation table, which produces level monthly payments. Escrow amounts are calculated annually, will generally change once per year and are added to the monthly level of principal and interest payment.

The way the bank establishes an *Ijara* transaction is that it is assumed that the bank has not made an interest-bearing loan. The bank would never loan any money that has to be paid back, rather they buy a property directly for the client's use. The client commits to buy the property from the bank over time, while also paying rent to use the property that the client does not yet own. Banks have designed *Ijara* transactions to resemble economically a conventional mortgage loan to the closest extent possible. This makes it easier to understand and compare and makes sure that the clients are getting a fair deal and allows them to budget for predictable payments. However, the mechanism by which banks produce this similarity to a simple conventional mortgage loan is complex.

Payments under the Purchase Commitment – this being one of the two *Ijara* documents normally involved – are made according to a schedule attached to the Commitment. These payments increase over time by a calculated amount, and are similar to the principal portion of a conventional mortgage payment.

Payments under the lease – the other *Ijara* document – consist of two components: an 'A' component rent and a 'B' component rent. The *Sharia'a* requires that the bank bear certain obligations of ownership. However, the costs of those obligations can be charged to the client as rent. The 'B' component rent covers these obligations, and approximates the same costs as the escrow items for a conventional mortgage plus the insurance needed to maintain the ownership structure of the property (one of the only additional costs associated with an *Ijara* that is not necessary for a conventional mortgage loan). These amounts would be paid by a conventional renter, but they would not be separated out – the landlord would simply base the rent on an amount designed to cover these costs. For the purpose of clarity a bank divides these amounts out as the 'B' component rent and adjusts this amount each year to be an accurate reflection of the actual costs.

The 'A' component rent covers the bank's compensation for participating in the transaction – just as a traditional landlord has costs to bear and maintain a property that is rented to the client (often by making payments on a conventional interest-bearing loan), which must be earned back from the rental. In addition, a landlord wants to make a profit on the transaction where the landlord's own money is invested in the building ownership. All these items will also be calculated into the rent the landlord charges the renter. In the bank's case, maintenance costs are paid by the client directly (or included in the 'B' component rent). The 'A' component rent is based on the cost to the bank of having its money invested in owning the property instead of in some other investment. The 'A' component rent is calculated in relation to interest rates, but it is a rental payment based on the client's use of the bank's property that the bank owns instead of owning a different interest-bearing investment.

The *Ijara* lease establishes a base 'A' component rent. This rental payment is based on an amount assuming the client has not paid any money at all towards ownership of the property. Because the bank requires the client to make an initial down-payment, the client will never pay this amount. The client will never pay this amount because the base rent is discounted based on how much the client has paid towards eventual ownership of the property. The listed rent merely serves as the number from which this discount is subtracted.

One way to think about this is as follows. The property renter is going to pay the same amount of rent every month. However, if the client not only rents the property, but actually owned part of the property as well, then any rent paid would be divided by the property owners in an amount related to each owner's percentage of ownership—thus the client would essentially be paying as renter part of the rent to himself as owner. Although the client will not own the property until all payments are made, the bank credits the client under the lease as if the client did have an ownership interest equal to the amount the client has paid towards eventual ownership and, instead of collecting the full rent and paying the client back his share, the bank simply charges the client his share of the rent owed.

As the client make payments under the Purchase Commitment, his 'ownership credit' (the rent discount) applied on the lease increases, and thus the amount of 'A' component rent the client owes each month decreases. A bank's *Ijara* products are designed so that if the client adds the payment due on the Purchase Commitment and the payment due on the lease together, it will produce a level monthly payment.

As mentioned, the 'B' component rent will change each year, but a new 'B' component rent will only produce a different level monthly payment – the payment will still be the same from one month to the next. These level payments can become 'decoupled,' and thus no longer stay even, in some circumstances. If the client's particular arrangement allows for the 'A' component rent to change, then once it changes the Purchase Commitment amount (which never changes from the original schedule given to the client when the documents are signed) added to the new 'A' component rent under the lease will no longer produce an even monthly payment – it will change each month. Additionally, if the client pays extra money towards ownership at any point, the client will be given a matching credit on the lease, which will cause the rent payment to be lower than was anticipated in calculating the payment schedule attached to the Purchase Commitment – which is designed to produce a level monthly payment.

In the end, although the mechanism for arriving at the payment amounts is quite complex, it is designed to be virtually identical to those the client would pay if he has a conventional mortgage loan – but without having to pay the conventional *haram* loan interest.

8. What are the advantages of *Ijara wa Iqtina* as compared to *Murabaha* as regards home finance?

The following advantages of *Ijara* over *Murabaha* are usually stressed:

1. *Ijara* allows clients more flexibility in both selecting adjustable or fixed rental options, whereas *Murabaha* is only fixed rate.
2. *Ijara* gives clients greater redemption (pre-payment) flexibility, whereas some *Murabaha* transactions have limitations on pre-payments.
3. Ijara allows the bank, in an Islamically-compliant way, to sell the investment in the clients' property to investors, whereas a *Murabaha* receivable is only securitisable at the full price of the receivable and not at a discount. If securitised, at other than par, *Murabaha* receivables must be less than 50% of the pool.
4. *Ijara* is easily restructured to help a bank to overcome repayment problems whereas Murabaha is not easily restructured, except at a loss to someone.
5. There is a way to expand a leasehold estate to help consumers release imputed equity in a property with *Ijara*. This is not possible under the *Sharia'a* when *Murabaha* is being applied.

9. Summarise the key differences between conventional leasing and Islamic leasing.

The most important financial difference between Islamically permitted leasing and conventional financial leasing is that the leasing agency must own the leased object for the duration of an Islamic lease. Therefore, although leasing a car from a manufacturer or dealership may in principle be permitted (if the contract satisfies the other conditions), some issues may not be *Sharia'a* compliant.

In many cases, the dealership will in fact use a bank or other financial intermediary to provide a loan for the present value of lease payments, and charge the customer interest on the loan. This would constitute the forbidden *riba*.

Diligent Islamic financial institutions would ensure that the contract abides by all the restrictions set out in the *Sharia'a* (e.g., sub-leasing requires the permission of the lessor, late payment penalties must be handled very carefully to avoid the forbidden *riba*, etc.).

10. Outline the key characteristics of Diminishing *Musharaka* as a technique for home finance.

Diminishing *Musharaka* is a special form of *Musharaka*. It ultimately culminates in the ownership of the asset or the project by the client. It operates in the following manner.

An Islamic bank participates as a financial partner. An agreement is signed by the partner and the bank that stipulates each party's share of the profits. However, the agreement also provides payment for a portion of the net income of the project as repayment of the principal financed by the bank. The partner is entitled to keep the rest. In this way, the bank's share of the equity is progressively reduced and the partner eventually becomes the full owner.

When a bank enters into a Diminishing *Musharaka* its intention is not to stay in the partnership until the arrangement is dissolved. In this type of partnership, the bank agrees to accept payment on an instalment basis or in one lump sum of an amount necessary to buy the bank's partnership interest. In this way, as the bank receives payments over and above its share in partnership profits, its partnership interest reduces until it is completely bought out of the partnership.

After the final payment the bank withdraws its claims from the partnership and the property becomes the property of the partner.

11. Summarise the key differences between *Ijara wa Iqtina* and Diminishing *Musharaka* as techniques for home finance.

In contrast to the *Ijara*/leasing model, where ownership of the financed item remains with the lessor for the entire lease period, ownership in a Diminishing *Musharaka* is explicitly shared between the customer and the Islamic financial institution (legally, what is established is an Islamic *Sharikat Al-Milk*).

The periodic payments of the customer in the Diminishing *Musharaka* model contain two parts: (i) a rental payment for the part of the property owned by the Islamic financial institution; and (ii) a buy-out of part of that reflecting ownership.

Over time, the portion of the asset that is owned by the customer increases, until he owns the entire asset and needs to pay no more rent. At that time, the contract is terminated.

So, under both methods the customer owns the building at the end of the period and makes rental and capital payments on the way. Does that mean that *Ijara wa Iqtina* and Diminishing *Musharaka* are the same?

No. With *Ijara*, ownership transfers at the end of the payment stream and with Diminishing *Musharaka*, ownership changes with each payment.

In *Ijara*, any payments are rent and 'on account' payments – payment being set aside until the moment in the future when the client converts his pool of on-account payments into the actual purchase. However, the client does not get title until he has made all the payments.

With *Ijara*, the promise to buy is a unilateral promise that the customer will buy in the future, and money is being set aside for that eventuality. It is not an agreement to buy now for which payments are being made now and over time.

Diminishing *Musharaka* changes the balance of ownership with each payment, but it also brings with it a different liability structure. The liability structure involves issues about who bears the risk of loss. For *Ijara*, the bank needs the owner's insurance; the tenant needs to be a coinsured or needs a renter's policy.

CASE STUDY 7: SOURCES OF FINANCE FOR ISLAMIC BANKS

Case Answers

Answers to Questions 1 and 2 are contained in the following tables.

1. Total returns to the bank	
Islamic financing	200,000
Provisions for losses	25,000
Revenues to be allocated	175,000

2. Total returns to the investment account holder				
	Bank (%)	**Bank share**	**Investor (%)**	
175,000	15	26,250	85	148,750
175,000	20	35,000	80	140,000
175,000	25	43,750	75	131,250
175,000	30	52,500	70	122,500
175,000	35	61,250	65	113,750

CASE STUDY 8: FINANCIAL STATEMENT ANALYSIS FOR ISLAMIC BANKS

No answers are provided for the questions in this case. Instead, readers should input the data into an Excel spreadsheet and undertake their own manipulations.

CASE STUDY 9: ISLAMIC INVESTMENT PROHIBITIONS

Case Answers

1. Would it be acceptable to finance food products whose ingredients are unknown?
   Not necessarily. The financier is expected to undertake due diligence to ascertain where the money is being invested. This is an issue that must be put to the *Sharia'a* Board for a ruling.

2. Would it be the duty of a bank financing food production to keep a list of reputable and reliable institutions that are qualified to classify food products as *halal*?
   No. This is an issue that must be put to the *Sharia'a* Board for a ruling.

3. What happens in the case of a client who contends that the religious school to which he subscribes allows him to purchase, consume and sell products containing gelatine produced from non-*halal* sources? The argument here being that the religious school is of the opinion that the original material used to produce the gelatine is totally transformed within the production process?
   This is an issue that must be put to the *Sharia'a* Board for a ruling.

4. Since the *Qur'an* prohibits assisting others in sin and evil, would an Islamic bank be allowed to finance the following:
   A. Equipment used to produce wine, which also is used for non-alcoholic drinks?
   B. Catering equipment for a company that primarily produces *haram* food products, which are to be sold to non-Muslims?
   These are issues that must be put to the *Sharia'a* Board for a ruling.

5. Can an Islamic bank finance an importer who wishes to purchase shoes with a pigskin lining, which are to be sold to non-Muslims?
   No.

6. Is it permissible to invest in a holding company when the Islamic status of the subsidiary company's income is unknown?
   This is an issue that must be put to the *Sharia'a* Board for a ruling.

7. What should be done in regard to interest earned on accounts in cases where money had to be held in bank accounts, due to business or safety reasons?
   This income is *haram*. It is a very grave sin for Muslims to profit from interest earnings.

8. Can interest be used to pay taxes in non-Muslim states?
   No. If interest earned is used in paying income tax or any other government taxes, it amounts to using it for personal benefit, hence it is not permissible. It is a very grave sin for Muslims to profit from interest earnings.

9. Can interest be used by the account holder or person who received it to pay other interest payments that are due e.g. interest on a mortgage or other loan?
   No. If the amount of interest is used in paying other interest payments it amounts to using it for personal benefit, hence it is not permissible. It is a very grave sin for Muslims to profit from interest earnings.

10. Can interest be used by poor Muslims who have no other sources of income?
    Yes – sometimes. Interest earnings can only be given as *Sadaqah* to those entitled to receive *zakat* and the *Sadaqah* can only be performed through *Tamlik*, i.e., by making the payee owner of the amount. However, interest earnings can be given to a poor person entitled to receive *zakat*. But unlike the *zakat* money, the amount of interest can also be given to a poor non-Muslim who does not have assets to the value of the *nisab* (threshold).

If they are so poor that they do not reach the *nisab* of *zakat*, the interest money can be given to them.

11. Should interest earned or received be returned to the very same institution that provided the interest?

No. The interest earnings can only be given as *Sadaqah* to those entitled to receive *zakat* and the *Sadaqah* can only be performed through *Tamlik*, i.e., by making the payee owner of the amount. So this amount cannot be given to any welfare scheme where it is spent in office expenditure, salaries of the staff, construction of buildings or purchasing things of public use without giving it in the ownership of a particular person. The institution providing interest earnings would not qualify to be repaid it under the *Tamlik* ruling.

12. Should money be kept in the bank, for safety reasons, and thereby inadvertently earn interest?

Any interest earned must be purified.

13. What happens in the case of persons who are compelled to pay interest on loans, taken out to fulfil normal economic necessities, which are absolutely essential for the purpose of economic reasons or survival, e.g., buying a car or house on interest?

Given the wider availability of Islamic finance, Muslims should strive to find an Islamic solution.

14. Would it be justifiable to buy a house on an interest basis when one can rent premises? What would the ruling be if renting the premises is not economically viable and the exorbitant rentals would prevent one from gaining the capacity to eventually purchase a property or other premises?

Given the wider availability of Islamic finance Muslims, should strive to find an Islamic solution.

15. Can Muslims charge non-Muslims interest or are Muslims prohibited from charging everyone interest irrespective of race or religion?

In whatever shape it comes, interest is *haram*.

16. Is interest only prohibited on loans for everyday daily spending or does the prohibition cover loans for generating further income using the finance for trade and investment?

In whatever shape it comes, interest is *haram*, according to the *Qur'an*.

17. What are the religious implications for Muslim accountants, lawyers and others who have to witness and record interest transactions?

In whatever shape they come, interest-related activities are *haram*, according to the *Qur'an*.

18. Can a Muslim investment consultant advise non-Muslim clients to invest in activities where their income would generate interest?

In whatever shape they come, interest-related activities are *haram*, according to the *Qur'an*.

19. Can Muslims buy assets, through interest-financing mechanisms, purely to evade taxation?

In whatever shape they come, interest-related activities are *haram*, according to the *Qur'an*.

20. Can interest earned on bank accounts be offset against bank charges?

In whatever shape they come, interest-related activities are *haram*, according to the *Qur'an*. However, interest-related stocks can have the interest-related proportion purified.

21. Why should interest remain prohibited when it is well known that inflation eats into its purchase value?

In whatever shape they come, interest-related activities are *Haram* according to the *Qur'an*.

22. Are any earnings acquired through the use of money borrowed on an interest basis, say through owning equities with debt in their balance sheet, also classified as prohibited in Islam?

Yes. In whatever shape they come, interest-related activities are *Haram*, according to the *Qur'an*.

23. Can a Muslim trade with another Muslim or non-Muslim whose earnings are from interest or other Islamically prohibited avenues?

Yes – subject to his conscience.

24. What should a convert to Islam do in respect of previous earnings from interest?

The earnings should be purified.

25. Assume that a Muslim had earned interest from particular investments. He was ignorant of the fact that investing in particular portfolios also implied the earning of interest through specific financial instruments. What should he do subsequent to gaining awareness in this regard?

The earnings should be purified.

26. Can any earned interest be given to non-Muslim charities such as blood banks, heart associations, community service groups, welfare committees for the aged, sick and disabled, and similar other disadvantaged groups?

No. Interest earnings can only be given as *Sadaqah* to those entitled to receive *zakat* and the *Sadaqah* can only be performed through *Tamlik*, i.e., by making the payee owner of the amount. So, this amount cannot be given to any welfare scheme where it is spent in office expenditure, salaries of the staff, construction of building or purchasing things of public use, without giving it in the ownership of a particular person.

27. Are beggars on the street entitled to be given any earned interest?

Yes

28. Given that there are many non-Muslims living under very low incomes, would they be preferable as recipients of any earned interest?

Interest earnings can only be given as *Sadaqah* to those entitled to receive it. Interest earnings can be given to poor people entitled to receive *zakat*.

Unlike the *zakat* money, the amount of interest can also be given to poor non-Muslims who do not reach the *nisab* (threshold). If they are so poor that they do not reach the *nisab* of *zakat*, the interest earnings can be given to them.

29. Is it acceptable to give any earned interest to
A. Build toilets in mosques?
B. Help counter anti-Muslim propaganda in the media?
C. Build mosques?

Interest earnings can only be given as *Sadaqah* to those entitled to receive *zakat* and the *Sadaqah* can only be performed through *Tamlik*, i.e., by making the payee owner of the amount. So, this amount cannot be given to any welfare scheme where it is spent in office expenditure, salaries of the staff, construction of building or purchasing things of public use, without giving it in the ownership of a particular person.

Sadaqah must be performed through *Tamlik*. So the money cannot be used for making toilets for a mosque or in the general expenditure of a Muslim association or countering propaganda. Nor can it be used to build mosques.

CASE STUDY 10: OPENING AN ISLAMIC BANK WITHIN A WESTERN REGULATORY FRAMEWORK

No answers are provided for the questions in this case because the answers are clearly provided within the case text.

CASE STUDY 11: LEVERAGE AND ISLAMIC BANKING

Case Answers

The answers to Questions 1.1 to 1.5 are contained in Table 11.1 (in bold).

Table 11.1

Debt ratio (%)	0	10	20	30	40	50	60	70	80	90
Capital										
Debt	0	100	200	300	400	500	600	700	800	900
Equity	1000	900	800	700	600	500	400	300	200	100
Total	1000	1000	1000	1000	1000	1000	1000	1000	1000	1000
Shares @ $10	100K	90K	80K	70K	60K	50K	40K	30K	20K	10K
Revenue	1000	1000	1000	1000	1000	1000	1000	1000	1000	1000
Cost/expense	800	800	800	800	800	800	800	800	800	800
EBIT	200	200	200	200	200	200	200	200	200	200
Interest	0	10	20	30	40	50	60	70	80	90
EBT	200	190	180	170	160	150	140	130	120	110
Tax	80	76	72	68	64	60	56	52	48	44
EAT	120	114	108	102	96	90	84	78	72	66
ROE	12.0%	12.7%	13.5%	14.6%	16.0%	18.0%	21.0%	26.0%	36.0%	66.0%
EPS	1.20	1.27	1.35	1.46	1.60	1.80	2.10	2.60	3.60	6.60
Interest rate	10%									
Tax rate	40%									

The answer to Question 2 is shown in Figure A11.1.
The answers to Questions 3.1 to 3.5 are contained in Table 11.2 (in bold).

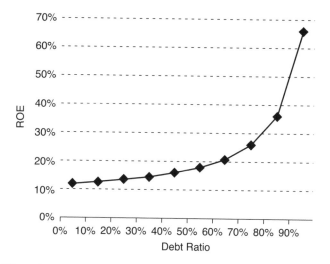

Figure A11.1   Effect of leverage on ROE

Table 11.2

Capital										
Debt	0	0	0	0	0	0	0	0	0	0
Equity	1000	1000	1000	1000	1000	1000	1000	1000	1000	1000
Total	1000	1000	1000	1000	1000	1000	1000	1000	1000	1000
Shares @ $10	100K	100K	100K	100K	100K	100K	100K	100K	100K	100K
Revenue	1000	1000	1000	1000	1000	1000	1000	1000	1000	1000
Cost/expense	800	800	800	800	800	800	800	800	800	800
EBIT	200	200	200	200	200	200	200	200	200	200
Interest	0	0	0	0	0	0	0	0	0	0
EBT	200	200	200	200	200	200	200	200	200	200
Tax	80	80	80	80	80	80	80	80	80	80
EAT	120	120	120	120	120	120	120	120	120	120
ROE	12.0%	12.0%	12.0%	12.0%	12.0%	12.0%	12.0%	12.0%	12.0%	12.0%
EPS	1.20	1.20	1.20	1.20	1.20	1.20	1.20	1.20	1.20	1.20
Interest rate	0%									
Tax rate	40%									

No answer is given here for Question 4 because the information is clearly provided within the case text.

CASE STUDY 12: IMPACT OF NON-PERFORMING LOANS ON ISLAMIC AND CONVENTIONAL BANKS

Case Answers

Answers to Questions 1 to 5 are contained in the following tables.

1. What is the initial balance sheet/profit and loss statement for each bank, after being fully capitalised?

Islamic bank			Conventional bank		
Initial balance sheet	Liabilities	Assets	Initial balance sheet	Liabilities	Assets
Capital	50		Capital	50	
Investment accounts	750		Deposits	750	
Total	800	800	Total	800	800

2. How do the profits made, and interest paid, change the income statement for each bank?

Islamic bank		Conventional bank	
Income statement		Income statement	
Revenues	88	Revenues	88
Interest costs	0	Interest costs	75
Net	88	Net	13

3. How do the financial statements compare after allowing for non-performing loans?

Islamic bank		Conventional bank	
Income statement		Income statement	
Revenues	88	Revenues	88
Interest costs	0	Interest costs	75
Net	88	Net	13
Capital Loss	−40	Capital Loss	−40
Net	48	Net	−27
		Taken from capital	−23

4. Assuming that the Islamic bank pays out all its profits, what is the payout to its depositors?

Islamic bank	
Income statement	
Revenues	88
Interest costs	0
Net	88
Capital Loss	−40
Net	48
Pays to depositors/shareholders 48/800 = 6%	

5. What are the prospects for both banks after adjustments of the financial statements for the non-performing loans?

Islamic bank			Conventional bank		
Initial balance sheet	**Liabilities**	**Assets**	**Initial balance sheet**	**Liabilities**	**Assets**
Capital	50		Capital	50	
Investment accounts	750		Deposits	750	
Total	800	800	Total	800	800
Solvent Bank			Solvent Bank		
Assets fall by 40			**Assets fall by 40**		
New Balance Sheet			**New Balance Sheet**		
Islamic Bank			**Conventional Bank**		
Capital	50		Capital	50	
Investment accounts	710		Deposits	750	
Total	760	760	Total	800	760
Solvent Bank			Insolvent Bank		

Following the adjustment for the non-performing loans the conventional bank is insolvent whilst the Islamic bank remains solvent.

Glossary

This glossary provides the key terms used in Islamic banking and finance. (A bold/italic term in a definition indicates that the word is defined elsewhere in the Glossary.)

Amanah: This refers to deposits held in trust. A person can hold a property in trust for another, sometimes by express contract and sometimes by implication of a contract. *Amanah* entails an absence of liability for loss except in the breach of duty. Current accounts are regarded as *Amanah* (trust). If the bank gets authority to use current accounts funds in its business, *Amanah* transforms into a loan. As every loan has to be repaid, banks are liable to repay the full amount of the current accounts.

Arbun: Down payment. A non-refundable deposit paid by a buyer retaining a right to confirm or cancel the sale.

Bai' Muajjal: Literally this means a credit sale. Technically, it is a financing technique adopted by Islamic banks that takes the form of **Murabaha** *Muajjal*. It is a contract in which the seller earns a profit margin on his purchase price and allows the buyer to pay the price of the commodity at a future date in a lump sum or in instalments. He has to mention expressly the cost of the commodity and the margin of profit is mutually agreed upon.

Bai' al-'Inah: A contract that involves the sale and buy-back transaction of assets by a seller. A seller sells the asset to a buyer on a cash basis. The seller later buys back the same asset on a deferred payment basis where the price is higher than the cash price.

Bai' al-Istijrar: A contract between the client and the supplier, whereby the supplier agrees to supply a particular produce on an ongoing basis, for example monthly, at an agreed price and on the basis of an agreed mode of payment.

Bai' al-Dayn: A transaction that involves the sale and purchase of securities or debt certificates that complies with the **Sharia'a**. Securities or debt certificates will be issued by a debtor to a creditor as evidence of indebtedness.

Bai' al-Muzayadah: An action by a person to sell an asset in the open market, which is accompanied by the process of bidding among potential buyers. The asset for sale will be awarded to the person who has offered the highest price.

Bai' bil Wafa: Sale with a right of the seller enabling him to repurchase (redeem) the property by refunding the purchase price. According to the majority of *Fuqaha* this is not permissible.

Bai' Bithaman Ajil (BBA): A contract that refers to the sale and purchase transactions for the financing of assets on a deferred and an instalment basis with a pre-agreed payment period. The sale price will include a profit margin.

Dayn (debt): A *Dayn* comes into existence as a result of a contract or credit transaction. It is incurred by way of rent, sale, purchase or in any other way that leaves it as a debt to another. *Duyun* (debts) should be repaid without any profit to the lender because they are advanced to help the needy and meet their demands and, therefore, the lender should not impose on the borrower more than he was given on credit.

Dhaman: Contract of guarantee, security or collateral.

Family Takaful: This arrangement provides members, or their beneficiaries, with financial protection: they will be provided with monetary benefits if they suffer a tragedy. Members can also enjoy long-term investment returns from the savings portion based on a pre-agreed ratio.

Fiqh: Islamic law. The science of the ***Sharia'a***. Practical jurisprudence or human articulations of divine rules encompassing both law and ethics. *Fiqh* may be understood as the Jurists' understanding of the ***Sharia'a***, or Jurists' law. *Fiqh al-Muamalat* is Islamic commercial jurisprudence, or the rules for transacting in a ***Sharia'a***-compliant manner. This is an important source of Islamic banking and economics.

Gharar: Any element of absolute or excessive uncertainty in any business or contract. *Gharar* potentially leads to undue loss to a party and unjustified enrichment of another. This is prohibited under the ***Sharia'a***.

Al Ghunm bil Ghurm: This provides the rationale and the principle of profit sharing in ***Shirkah*** arrangements. Earning profit is legitimised only by engaging in an economic venture involving risk sharing that ultimately contributes to economic development.

Halal: Anything permitted by the ***Sharia'a***.

Haram: Anything prohibited by the ***Sharia'a***.

Hawalah: Literally, this means transfer. Legally, it is an agreement by which a debtor is freed from a debt by another party becoming responsible for it or by the transfer of a claim of a debt shifting the responsibility from one person to another. It also refers to the document by which the transfer takes place.

Hibah: Gift.

Ijara: Leasing. This is the sale of a definite usufruct of any asset in exchange for definite reward. It refers to a contract under which Islamic banks lease equipment, buildings or other facilities to a client, against an agreed rental.

Ijara wa Iqtina: A mode of financing, by way of hire purchase, adopted by Islamic banks. It is a contract under which an Islamic bank finances equipment, buildings or other facilities for the client against an agreed rental together with a unilateral undertaking by the bank or the client that, at the end of the lease period, the ownership in the asset will be transferred to the lessee. The undertaking, or the promise, does not become an integral part of the lease contract in order to make it conditional. The rental, as well as the purchase price, is fixed in such a manner that the bank gets back its principal sum along with some profit. This is usually determined in advance.

Ijtihad: An endeavour of a qualified Jurist to derive or formulate a rule of law to determine the true ruling of the divine law in a matter on which the revelation is not explicit or certain. This would be on the basis of *Nass* (evidence) found in the *Qur'an* and the ***Sunnah***.

Ijma: Consensus of all or a majority of the leading qualified Jurists on a certain ***Sharia'a*** matter at a certain moment in time.

'Inah: A double sale by which the borrower and the lender sell and then resell an object between them, once for cash and once for a higher price on credit, with the net result being a loan with interest.

'Inan (type of *Sharikah*): A form of partnership in which each partner contributes capital and has a right to work for the business, not necessarily equally.

Istihsan: A doctrine of Islamic law that allows exceptions to strict legal reasoning, or guiding choice among possible legal outcomes, when considerations of human welfare so demand.

Istisna'a: A contractual agreement for manufacturing goods and commodities, allowing cash payment in advance and future delivery or a future payment and future delivery. A manufacturer or builder agrees to produce or build a well described good or building at a given price on a given date in the future. The price can be paid in instalments, step by step as agreed between the parties. *Istisna'a* can be used for financing the manufacture or construction of houses, plant, projects and the building of bridges, roads and power stations.

Iwad: An equivalent counter-value or recompense. This is an important principle of Islamic finance. Contracts without *iwad* are not Islamically acceptable.

Jahala: Ignorance, lack of knowledge; indefiniteness in a contract, sometimes leading to *gharar*.

Jua'alah: Literally, *Jua'alah* constitutes wages, pay, stipend or reward. Legally, it is a contract for performing a given task against a prescribed fee in a given period. *Ujrah* is a similar contract in which any work is done against a stipulated wage or fee.

Kafalah (suretyship): Literally, *Kafalah* means responsibility, or suretyship. Legally in *Kafalah* a third party becomes a surety for the payment of debt. It is a pledge given to a creditor that the debtor will pay the debt or fine. Suretyship in Islamic law is the creation of an additional liability with regard to the claim, not to the debt itself.

Khiyar: Option or a power to annul or cancel a contract.

Maisir: An ancient Arabian game of chance played with arrows without heads and feathers, for stakes of slaughtered and quartered camels. It came to be identified with all types of gambling.

al-masnoo: The subject matter of an *Istisna'a* contract.

al-musania'a: The seller/manufacturer in an *Istisna'a* contract.

al-muslam: The buyer in a *Salam* contract.

al-muslam fihi: The commodity to be delivered in a *Salam* contract.

al-muslam ileihi: The seller in a *Salam* contract.

al-mustasni: The ultimate buyer in an *Istisna'a* contract.

Mithli (fungible goods): Goods that can be returned in kind, that is gold for gold, silver for silver, US$ for US$, wheat for wheat and so on.

Mujtahid: Legal expert, or a Jurist who expends great effort in deriving a legal opinion interpreting the sources of *Sharia'a* law.

Mudaraba (trust financing): An agreement made between two parties one of whom provides 100% of the capital for the project and who has no control over the management of the project, and another party know as a *Mudarib*, who manages the project using his entrepreneurial skills. Profits arising from the project are distributed according to a predetermined ratio. Losses are borne by the provider of capital.

Mudarib: The managing partner in a *Mudaraba* contract.

Mujir: The lessor – a person or institution who provides an asset with an *Ijara* (lease).

Murabaha (cost plus financing): A contract sale between the bank and its client for the sale of goods at a price that includes a profit margin agreed by both parties. As a financing technique it involves the purchase of goods by the bank as requested by its client. The goods are sold to the client with an agreed mark-up.

Musawamah: A general kind of sale in which the price of the commodity to be traded is arrived at by bargaining between the seller and the purchaser without any reference to the price paid or cost incurred by the former.

Musharaka (joint venture financing): This Islamic financing technique involves a joint venture between two parties who both provide capital for the financing of a project. Both parties share profits on a pre-agreed ratio, but losses are shared on the basis of equity participation. Management of the project may be carried out by both the parties or by just one party. This is a very flexible arrangement where the sharing of the profits and management can be negotiated and pre-agreed by all parties.

Musharik: Professional who manages the transactions under the **Musharaka** mode of financing

Mustajir: The lessee – a person (or institution) to whom an asset with an **Ijara** (lease) is provided.

Mutajara: Deposits made by banks in Saudi Arabia to SAMA, the central bank.

Muwakkil: The person who appoints the **Wakil** in a **Wakala** contract.

Qard (loan of fungible objects): Legally, *Qard* means to give something of value without expecting any return. *Qard* can provide help, charity or money needed for a specific occasion (death, wedding and so on). No monetary return is expected although the finance must be repaid. The Prophet is reported to have said '. . . every loan must be paid. . .'. But if a debtor is in difficulty, the creditor is expected to extend time or even voluntarily remit the whole or a part of the principal. The literal meaning of *Qard* is to cut. It is so called because the property is really cut off when it is given to the borrower.

Qimar: Gambling. Technically, it is an arrangement in which possession of something of value is contingent upon the happening of an uncertain event. By implication it applies to a situation in which there is a loss for one party and a gain for the other without specifying which party will lose and which will gain.

Qiyas: Literally, this means measure, example, comparison or analogy. Technically, it means a derivation of the law on the analogy of an existing law if the basis (*'ilaih*) of the two is the same. It is one of the sources of **Sharia'a** law.

Rab ul Mall: Capital investor/finance provider.

Rahn: (pledge or collateral). Legally, *Rahn* means to pledge or lodge a real or corporeal property of material value, in accordance with the law, as security, for a debt or pecuniary obligation so as to make it possible for the creditor to recover the debt or some portion of the goods or property. In the pre-Islamic contracts, *Rahn* implied a type of 'earnest money', which was lodged as a guarantee and material evidence or proof of a contract, especially when there was no scribe available to confirm this in writing.

Ras ul Mall: Capital (cost) paid (in cash, kind or benefit) in both **Salam** and **Istisna'a** contracts; i.e., the price paid.

Riba: An excess or increase. Technically, it means an increase over principal in a loan transaction or in exchange for a commodity accrued to the owner (lender) without giving an equivalent counter-value or recompense (*'iwad*), in return, to the other party. *Riba* means an increase that is without an *'iwad* or equal counter-value.

Riba Al-Fadl: '*Riba* in excess': the quality premium when exchanging low quality with better quality goods, for example, dates for dates, wheat for wheat and so on. In other words, an excess in the exchange of *Ribawi* goods within a single genus. The concept of *Riba Al-Fadl* refers to sale transactions while **Riba Al-Nasiah** refers to loan transactions.

Riba Al-Nasiah: *'Riba* of delay' is due to an exchange not being immediate with or without excess in one of the counter-values. It is an increment on the principal of a loan or debt payable, and refers to the practice of lending money for any length of time on the understanding that the borrower will return to the lender, at the end of the period, the amount originally lent together with an increase on it, in consideration of the lender having granted him time to pay. Interest, in all modern conventional banking transactions, falls under the purview of *Riba Al-Nasiah*. As money in the present banking system is exchanged for money with excess and delay, it falls under the definition of *riba*. There is a general accord reached among scholars that *riba* is prohibited under **Sharia'a** law.

Sadaqah: Deeds of giving, charitable donations, alms and so on.

Sahib-ul-Mal: Under the **Mudaraba Takaful** model, the entrepreneur (or **Mudarib** – the **Takaful** operator) accepts payment of the **Takaful** instalments or **Takaful** contributions premium (termed the **Ras ul Mall**) from investors or providers of capital or fund (**Takaful** participants) acting as *Sahib-ul-Mal*.

Salaf (loan/debt): Literally, a loan that draws forth no profit for the creditor. In a wider sense this includes loans for specified periods; that is, for short, intermediate and long term loans. *Salaf* is another name for **Salam** wherein the price of the commodity is paid in advance while the commodity or the counter-value is supplied in the future. Thus the contract creates a liability for the seller.

Salam: A contract in which advance payment is made for goods to be delivered later. The seller undertakes to supply some specific goods to the buyer at a future date in exchange for a price fully paid in advance at the time of contract. According to the normal rules of the **Sharia'a**, no sale can be affected unless the goods are in existence at the time of the contract. However *Salam* forms an exception, given by the Prophet, to the general rule provided the goods are defined and the date of delivery is fixed. It is necessary that the quality of the commodity intended to be purchased is fully specified leaving no ambiguity potentially leading to a dispute. The objects of the *Salam* sale are goods and cannot be gold, silver or currencies. The latter are regarded as monetary values, the exchange of which is covered under rules of **Sarf**, that is mutual exchange should be hand to hand (spot) without delay. With this latter exception, *Salam* covers almost everything capable of being definitively described as to quantity, quality and workmanship.

Sarf: Basically, in pre-Islamic times this was the exchange of gold for gold, silver for silver and gold for silver or vice versa. In **Sharia'a** law such exchange is regarded as sale of price for price (*Bai al Thaman bil Thaman*), and each price is consideration of the other. *Sarf* also means the sale of monetary value for monetary value, meaning foreign exchange transactions.

Sharia'a: The term *Sharia'a* has two meanings: Islamic Law and the totality of divine categorisations of human acts (Islam). *Sharia'a* rules do not always function as rules of law in the Western sense, because they include obligations, duties and moral considerations not generally thought of as 'law'. *Sharia'a* rules, therefore, admitting of both a legal and moral dimension, have as their purpose the fostering of obedience to Allah the Almighty. In the legal terminology, *Sharia'a* means the law as extracted by the **Mujtahid** from the sources of law.

Shirkah: A contract between two or more persons who launch a business or financial enterprise to make profits. In the conventional books of **Fiqh**, the partnership business may include both **Musharaka** and **Mudaraba**.

Sukuk: Islamic bonds, similar to asset-backed bonds.

Sunnah: Custom, habit or way of life. Technically, this refers to the utterances of the Prophet Mohammed other than the *Qur'an*, being known as the *Hadith*, or his personal acts, or sayings of others, tacitly approved by the Prophet.

Tabarru': A donation or gift, the purpose of which is not commercial but is given in seeking the pleasure of Allah. Any benefit that is given by one person to another without getting something in exchange is called *Tabarru'*.

Takaful: A ***Sharia'a***-compliant system of insurance in which the participants donate part of or all of their contributions, which are used to pay claims for damages suffered by some of the participants. The *Takaful* operator's role is restricted to managing the insurance operations and investing the insurance contributions.

Tamlik: Complete and exclusive personal possession. The act of giving, in a *zakat* sense, is only complete, from an Islamic perspective, if there is a full transfer of ownership of the *zakat* donation.

Tapir: Spending wastefully on objects that have been explicitly prohibited by the ***Sharia'a***, irrespective of the amount of expenditure.

Wadia: System in which an Islamic bank acts as keeper and trustee of depositor funds.

Wakala: A contract of agency in which one person appoints someone else to perform a certain task on his behalf, usually against a certain fee.

Wakil: The agent appointed by the ***Muwakkil*** in a ***Wakala*** contract.

Waqf: An Islamic endowment in which a particular property is set aside, in perpetuity, for a particular charity.

Zakat: Literally, this means blessing, purification, increase or cultivation of good deeds. It is a religious obligation of alms-giving, on a Muslim, to pay 2.5% of certain kinds of wealth annually to one of the eight categories of needy Muslims.

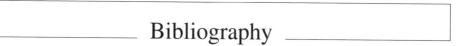

Bibliography

This text draws on a wide variety of references. In order to appreciate the central elements that lie at the heart of Islamic banking, readers are strongly urged to consult the following *Sura* from the *Qur'an*. The key references to *riba* can be found in

- Sura 2: 275–280
- Sura 3: 130
- Sura 4: 161
- Sura 30: 39

BOOKS

Ahmad, Ausaf and Khan, Tariqullah (1997). *Islamic Financial Instruments for Public Sector Resource Mobilization*, Jeddah, Saudi Arabia: IDB, IRTI.

Ahmad, Ausaf and Khan, Tariqullah (eds) (1998). *Islamic Financial Instruments for Public Sector Resource Mobilization*, Jeddah, Saudi Arabia: IRTI.

Ahmad, Khurshid (ed.) (1976). *Studies in Islamic Economics*, Leicester, UK: The Islamic Foundation.

Al-Harran, Saad Abdul Sattar (1993). *Islamic Finance: Partnership Financing*, Selangor, Malaysia: Pelanduk Publications.

Al-Harran, Saad Abdul Sattar (1995). *Leading Issues in Islamic Banking and Finance*, Selangor, Malaysia: Pelanduk Publications.

Ali, Syed Ameer (1978). *The Spirit of Islam: A History of the Evolution and Ideals of Islam, with a Life of the Prophet*, London, UK: Chatto & Windus.

Ali, S. Nazim and Ali, Naseem N. (1994). *Information Sources on Islamic Banking and Economics, 1980–1990*, Kegan Paul International.

al-Misri, Ahmad ibn Naqid (1988). *Reliance of the Traveller: A Classical Manual of Islamic Sacred Law*, Translation by Nuh Ha Mim Keller: Amana Publications.

Al-Omar, Fouad and Abdel Haq, Mohammed (1996). *Islamic Banking, Theory, Practice and Challenges*, London, UK: Oxford University.

al-Qaradawi, Yusuf (1985). *The Lawful and the Prohibited in Islam*, Kuala Lumpur, Malaysia: Islamic Book Trust.

Archer, Simon and Karim, Rifaat Abdel (2002). *Islamic Finance: Innovation and Growth*, London, UK: Euromoney Books and AAOIFI.

Ariff, Mohammad and Mannan, M.A. (1990). *Developing a System of Islamic Financial Instruments*, Jeddah, Saudi Arabia: IDB, IRTI.

Armstrong, Karen (2002). *Islam: A Short History*, New York, USA: Modern Library (revised edn).

Ayub, Mohammad (2002). *Islamic Banking and Finance: Theory and Practice*, Karachi, Pakistan: State Bank Printing Press.

BenDjilali, Boualem and Khan, Tariqullah (1995). *Economics of Diminishing Musharakah*, Jeddah, Saudi Arabia: IRTI.

Bowker, John (1999). *What Muslims Believe*, Oxford, UK: OneWorld.

Burton, John (1990). *The Sources of Islamic Law: Islamic Theories of Abrogation*, Edinburgh, UK: Edinburgh University Press.

Burton, John (1994). *An Introduction to the Hadith*, Edinburgh, UK: Edinburgh University Press.

Chapra, M.U. (1985). *Towards a Just Monetary System*, Leicester, UK: The Islamic Foundation.

Chapra, M.U. (1992). *Islam and the Economic Challenge*, Leicester, UK: The Islamic Foundation.

Chapra, M.U. (2000). *The Future of Islamic Economics*, Leicester, UK: The Islamic Foundation.

Cook, Michael (2000). *The Koran: A Very Short Introduction*, Oxford, UK: Oxford University Press.

Cooter, Robert and Thomas Ulen (2000). *Law and Economics*, 3rd edition, Reading, MA, USA: Addison-Wesley.

Coulson, N.J. (1994). *A History of Islamic Law*, Edinburgh, UK: Edinburgh University Press.

De Lorenzo, Yusuf Talal (eds) (1997). *A Compendium of Legal Opinions on the Operations of Islamic Banks: Murabahah, Mudarabah and Musharakah*, London, UK: Institute of Islamic Banking and Insurance.

El-Gamal, M.A. (2003). *A Basic Guide to Contemporary Islamic Banking and Finance*, elgamal@rice.edu http://www.ruf.rice.edu/~elgamal

El-Gamal, M.A. (2003). *Financial Transactions in Islamic Jurisprudence*, Vols 1 and 2, Translation by Dr Al-Zuhayli: kitaabun.com.

Esposito, John L. (1995). *The Oxford Encyclopedia of the Modern Islamic World*, 4 vols, Oxford, UK: Oxford University Press.

Farouqui, Mahmood (ed.) (1997). *Islamic Banking and Investment: Challenge and Opportunity*, Kegan Paul International.

Garrett, R. and Graham, A. (eds) (1998). *Islamic Law and Finance*, Introduction by William Ballantyne, London, UK: Graham & Trotman.

Hallaq, Wael B. (ed.) (2003). *The Formation of Islamic Law*, Aldershot, UK: Ashgate.

Haron, Sudin (1997). *Islamic Banking: Rules and Regulations*, Selangor, Malaysia: Pelanduk Publications.

Haron, Sudin and Bala Shanmugam (1997). *Islamic Banking System: Concepts and Applications*, Selangor, Malaysia: Pelanduk Publications.

Henry, C.M. and Rodney Wilson (eds) (2004). *Politics of Islamic Finance*, Edinburgh, UK: Edinburgh University Press.

Homoud, Sami Hassan (1985). *Islamic Banking*, London, UK: Arabian Information.

Homoud, S. (1985). *Islamic Banking*, London, UK: Graham & Trotman.

Institute of Islamic Banking and Insurance (1996). *Islamic Banking: An Overview*, London, UK: Institute of Islamic Banking and Insurance.

Institute of Islamic Banking and Insurance (2000). *International Directory of Islamic Banks and Institutions*, London, UK: Institute of Islamic Banking and Insurance.

International Association of Islamic Banks (1997). *Directory of Islamic Banks and Financial Institutions*, Jeddah, Saudi Arabia: International Association of Islamic Banks.

Iqbal, M. (ed.) (2002). *Islamic Banking and Finance*, Leicester, UK: The Islamic Foundation.

Iqbal, M. and Khan, Tariqullah (2005). *Financial Engineering and Islamic Contracts*, Basingstoke, UK: Palgrave-Macmillan.

Iqbal, M. and Molyneux, Philip (2005). *Thirty Years of Islamic Banking: History and Performance*, Basingstoke, UK: Palgrave-Macmillan.

Iqbal, Munawar and Llewellyn, David T. (2002). *Islamic Banking and Finance: New Perspectives in Profit Sharing and Risk*, London, UK: Edward Elgar Publishers.

Jaffer, S. (ed.) (2004). *Islamic Asset Management: Forming the Future for Sharia-Compliant Investment Strategies*, London, UK: Euromoney.

Kahf, Monzer and Khan, Tariqullah (1992). *Principles of Islamic Financing*, Jeddah, Saudi Arabia: IRTI.

Kamal, H. (2001). *Islamic Commercial Law: An Analysis of Futures and Options*, Cambridge, UK: Islamic Text Society.

Kamali, Mohammad Hashim (2000). *Principles of Islamic Jurisprudence*, Cambridge, UK: The Islamic Texts Society, revised edn.

Kettell, B. (1999). *Fed-watching: The impact of the Fed on the World's Financial Markets*, Financial Times-Prentice Hall.
Kettell, B. (1999). *What Drives Financial Markets?* Financial Times-Prentice Hall.
Kettell, B. (2000). *What drives the Currency Markets?* Financial Times-Prentice Hall.
Kettell, B. (2001). *Economics for Financial Market*, Butterworth's-Heinemann.
Kettell, B. (2001). *Financial Economics*, Financial Times-Prentice Hall.
Kettell, B. (2002). *Islamic Banking in the Kingdom of Bahrain*, Bahrain Monetary Agency (BMA).
Kettell, B. (2006). *Sukuk: a definitive guide to Islamic Structured Finance*, Thompson Hine.
Khan, M. Fahim (1996). *Islamic Futures and their Markets*, Jeddah, Saudi Arabia: IRTI.
Khan, Shahrukh Rafi (1988). *Profit and Loss Sharing: An Islamic Experiment in Finance and Banking*, Oxford, UK: Oxford University Press.
Khan, W.M. (1985). *Towards an Interest-Free Islamic Economic System*, Leicester, UK: The Islamic Foundation.
Lewis, Mervyn K. and Latifa M. Algaoud (2001). *Islamic Banking*, Cheltenham, UK: Edward Elgar.
Mehdi, Rubya (1994). *The Islamization of the Law in Pakistan*, Richmond, Surrey: Curzon Press.
Mills, Paul S. and John R. Presley (1999). *Islamic Finance: Theory and Practice*, London, UK: Macmillan.
Moore, Philip (1997). *Islamic Finance: A Partnership for Growth*, London, UK: Euromoney.
Rahman, Yahia Abdul (1994). *Interest Free Islamic Banking – Lariba Bank*, Kuala Lumpur, Malaysia: Al-Hilal Publishing.
Rosly, S.A. (2005). *Critical Issues in Islamic Banking and Financial Markets*, Bloomington, IN, USA: AuthorHouse.
Roy, O. (2004). *Globalised Islam, The Search for a New Ummah*, Huot & Co.
Saeed, Abdullah (1997). *Islamic Banking and Interest: A Study of the Prohibition of Ribā and Its Contemporary Interpretation*, 2nd edition, Leiden, The Netherlands: E.J. Brill.
Saleh, Nabil A. (1992). *Unlawful Gain and Legitimate Profit in Islamic Law*, 2nd edition, London, UK: Graham and Trotman.
Shirazi (1990). *Islamic Banking Contracts*, London, UK: Butterworth-Heinemann.
Siddiqi, M.N. (1983). *Issues in Islamic Banking*, Leicester, UK: The Islamic Foundation.
Siddiqi, M.N. (1985). *Partnership and Profit Sharing*, Leicester, UK: The Islamic Foundation.
Siddiqi, M.N. (1988). *Banking Without Interest*, Leicester, UK: The Islamic Foundation.
Udovitch, Abraham L. (1970) *Partnership and Profit in Medieval Islam*, Princeton, NJ, USA: Princeton University Press.
Usmani, M.T. (1998). *An Introduction to Islamic Finance*, Karachi, Pakistan: Idaratul-Ma'arif.
Usmani, M.T. (2000). *The Historic Judgment on Interest*, Karachi, Pakistan: Idaratul-Ma'arif.
Vogal, Frank E. and Samuel L. Hayes (1988). *Islamic Law and Finance: Religion, Risk and Return*, The Hague, The Netherlands: Kluwer Law International.
Warde, I. (2000). *Islamic Finance in the Global Economy*, Edinburgh, UK: Edinburgh University Press.
Zineldin, Mosad (1990), *The Economics of Money and Banking: A Theoretical and Empirical Study of Islamic Interest-Free Banking*, Stockholm, Sweden: Almqvist & Wiksell International.

AAOIFI PUBLICATIONS

AAOIFI (1999). *Statement on the Purpose and Calculation of the Capital Adequacy Ratio for Islamic Banks*, Manama, Bahrain: The Accounting & Auditing Organization for Islamic Financial Institutions.
AAOIFI (2002). *Accounting, Auditing and Governance Standards*, Manama, Bahrain: The Accounting & Auditing Organization for Islamic Financial Institutions.
AAOIFI (2002). *Investment Sukuk (Shari'ah Standard No.18)*, Manama, Bahrain: The Accounting & Auditing Organization for Islamic Financial Institutions.
AAOIFI (2003). *Shari'ah Standards*, Manama, Bahrain: The Accounting & Auditing Organization for Islamic Financial Institutions.
AAOIFI (2004). *Guiding Principles of Risk Management for Institutions* (Insurance companies offering only Islamic Financial Services), Manama, Bahrain: The Accounting & Auditing Organization for Islamic Financial Institutions.

AAOIFI (2004). *Capital Adequacy Standard for Institutions* (offering only Islamic Financial Services), Manama, Bahrain: The Accounting & Auditing Organization for Islamic Financial Institutions.

ARTICLES AND PAPERS

Abdallah, A. (1987). 'Islamic Banking', *Journal of Islamic Banking and Finance*, Jan–Mar, 4(1): 31–56.

Abdul, Majid and Abdul, Rais (2003). 'Development of Liquidity Management Instruments: Challenges and Opportunities', paper presented to the International Conference on Islamic Banking: Risk Management, Regulation and Supervision, held in Jakarta, Indonesia, 30 September–2 October 2003, organised by IRTI, Bank Indonesia and Ministry of Finance: Indonesia.

Abdul-Rahman, Yahla and Abdulah, S. Tug (1999). 'Towards a LARIBA (Islamic) Mortgage in the United States: Providing an Alternative to the Traditional Mortgages', *International Journal of Islamic Financial Services*, 1(2), Jul–Sep.

Aftab, M. (1986). 'Pakistan moves to Islamic banking', *The Banker*, June: 57–60.

Aggarwal, R.K. and Yousef, T. (2000). 'Islamic Banks and Investment Financing', *Journal of Money, Credit and Banking*, 32, 93–120.

Ahmad, Dr. Abdel Rahman Yousri (2001). 'Riba, its Economic Rationale and Implications', *New Horizon*, 109, May–June.

Ahmad, Ziauddin (1995). 'Islamic Banking: State of the Art', *IDB Prize Lecture*, Jeddah, Saudi Arabia: Islamic Research and Training Institute, Islamic Development Bank.

Alam, M.A. (2000). 'Islamic Banking in Bangladesh: A Case Study of IBBL', *International Journal of Islamic Financial Services*, 1(4), Jan–Mar.

Al-Bashir, M. and Muhammed al-Amine (2001). 'The Islamic Bonds Market: Possibilities and Challenges', *International Journal of Islamic Financial Services*, 3(1), Apr–Jun.

Al-Jarhi, Mabid Ali and Iqbal, Munawar (2001). 'Islamic Banking: FAQs', Occasional Paper #4, Jeddah, Saudi Arabia: Islamic Research and Training Institute.

Al-Suwailem, Sami (2000). 'Decision Under Uncertainty, An Islamic Perspective', in Islamic Finance: Challenges and Opportunities in the Twenty-First Century (Conference Papers). Loughborough: *Fourth International Conference on Islamic Economics and Banking*.

Anouar, H. (2002). 'Profitability of Islamic Banks', *International Journal of Islamic Financial Services*, 4(2), Jul–Sep.

Archer, S., Karim, R. Abdel and Al-Deehani, T. (1998). 'Financial Contracting, Governance Structures and the Accounting Regulation of Islamic Banks: An Analysis in Terms of Agency Theory and Transaction Cost Economics', *Journal of Management and Governance*, 2, 149–170.

Ariff, M. (1982). 'Monetary Policy in an Interest-Free Islamic Economy – Nature and Scope' in Ariff, M. (ed.). *Monetary and Fiscal Economics of Islam*, Jeddah, Saudi Arabia: International Centre for Research in Islamic Economics.

Ayub, Muhammad (1995). 'Meaning of Riba', *Journal of Islamic Banking and Finance*, 12(2).

Babikir, Osman Ahmed (2001). Islamic Financial Instruments to Manage Short-term Excess Liquidity, Research Paper No.41, 2nd edn, Jeddah, Saudi Arabia: Islamic Research and Training Institute.

Bacha, O.I. (1999). 'Financial Derivatives: Some Thoughts for Reconsideration', *International Journal of Islamic Financial Services*, 1(1), Apr–Jun.

Baldwin, K. (2002). 'Risk Management in Islamic Banks', in Karim, R. Abdel and Archer, S. (eds). *Islamic Finance: Innovation and Growth*, Euromoney Books and AAOIFI, pp. 176–197.

Basel Committee on Banking Supervision (BCBS) (2003). Consultative Document – Overview of the New Basel Capital Accord, Bank for International Settlements, April.

Bashir, A. (1996). 'Profit-sharing Contracts and Investment under Asymmetric Information', *Research in Middle East Economics*, 1, 173–186.

Buckmaster, Daphne (ed.) (1996). 'Central Bank Supervision: The Need for Unity', in *Islamic Banking: An Overview*, London: Institute of Islamic Banking and Insurance, pp. 143–145.

Buckmaster, Daphne, (ed.) (1996). 'Alternative Tools of Supervision by Central Banks', in *Islamic Banking: An Overview*, London: Institute of Islamic Banking and Insurance, pp. 146–150.

Chapra, M. Umer (1982). 'Money and Banking in an Islamic Economy', in Ariff, M. (ed.) *Monetary and Fiscal Economics of Islam*, Jeddah, Saudi Arabia: International Centre for Research in Islamic Economics.

Chapra, M. Umer (2000). 'Why has Islam Prohibited Interest?: Rationale Behind the Prohibition of Interest', *Review of Islamic Economics*, 9.

Chapra, M. Umer and Habib Ahmed (2002). Corporate Governance in Islamic Financial Institutions, Occasional Paper No. 6, Jeddah, Saudi Arabia: Islamic Research and Training Institute.

Chapra, M. Umer and Tariqullah Khan (2000). 'Regulation and Supervision of Islamic Banks', Occasional Paper No.3, Jeddah, Saudi Arabia: Islamic Development Bank – Islamic Research and Training Institute.

Cunningham, A. (2001). 'Culture of Accounting: What are the Real Constraints for Islamic Finance in a Riba-Based Global Economy?' London, UK: Moody's Investor Services.

Dale, Richard (2000). 'Comparative Models of Banking Supervision', paper presented to the *Conference on Islamic Banking Supervision*, Bahrain: AAOIFI, February.

Dar, H.A. and Presley, J.R. (1999). 'Islamic Finance: A Western Perspective', *International Journal of Islamic Financial Services*, 1(1), Apr–June.

Dar, H.A. and Presley, J.R. (2000). 'Lack of Profit Sharing in Islamic Banking: Management and Control Imbalances', *International Journal of Islamic Financial Services*, 2(2), Jul–Sep.

El-Din, A.K. (1986). 'Ten Years of Islamic Banking', *Journal of Islamic Banking and Finance*, Jul–Sep, 3(3): 49–66.

El-Gamal, Mahmoud (2000). 'An Economic Explication of the Prohibition of Gharar in Classical Islamic Jurisprudence', in Islamic Finance: Challenges and Opportunities in the Twenty First Century (Conference Papers). Loughborough: *Fourth International Conference on Islamic Economics and Banking*.

Elgari, M. Ali (1997). 'Short Term Financial Instruments Based on Salam Contracts', in Ausaf Ahmad and Tariqullah Khan (eds.). *Islamic Financial Instruments for Public Sector Resource Mobilization*, Jeddah, Saudi Arabia: Islamic Research and Training Institute, pp. 249–66.

El-Karanshawy, Hatem (1998). 'CAMEL Ratings and their Relevance for Islamic Banks', paper presented to a Seminar on Islamic Banking Supervision, organised by the Arab Monetary Fund: Abu Dhabi.

El Sheikkh, Fath El Rahman (2000). 'The Regulation of Islamic Banks by Central Banks', *The Journal of International Banking Regulation*, Fall, 43–49.

Errico, Luca, and Mitra Farahbaksh (1998). 'Islamic Banking: Issues in Prudential Regulations and Supervision', IMF Working Paper 98/30, Washington: International Monetary Fund.

Fadeel, Mahmoud (2002). 'Legal Aspects of Islamic Finance', in Archer, Simon and Karim, Rifaat Abdel (eds). *Islamic Finance: Growth and Innovation*, London, UK: Euromoney Books.

Gafoor, A.L.M. Abdul (2001). 'Mudaraba-based Investment and Finance', *New Horizon*, 110, July.

Gafoor, A.L.M. Abdul (2001). 'Riba-free Commercial Banking', *New Horizon*, 112, September.

Grais, W. and Kantur, Z. (2003). 'The Changing Financial Landscape: Opportunities and Challenges for the Middle East and North Africa', *World Bank Policy Research Working Paper* 3050, May 2003.

Haque, Nadeemul and Abbas Mirakhor (1999). 'The Design of Instruments for Government Finance in an Islamic Economy', *Islamic Economic Studies*, 6(2): 27–43.

Haron, S. and Norafifah Ahmad (2000). 'The Effects of Conventional Interest Rates on Funds Deposited with Islamic Banking System in Malaysia', *International Journal of Islamic Financial Services*, 1(4), Jan–Mar.

Hassan, Sabir Mohammad (2000). 'Capital Adequacy and Basel Guidelines: On Risk Weights of Assets for Islamic Banks', paper presented at the Conference on the Regulation of Islamic Banks, in Bahrain, February.

Hoque, M.Z. and Masdul Alam Choudhury (2003). 'Islamic Finance: A Western Perspective Revisited', International *Journal of Islamic Financial Services*, 4(4), Apr–June.

Ibrahim, Tag El-Din S. (1991). 'Risk Aversion, Moral Hazard and Financial Islamization Policy', *Review of Islamic Economics*, 1(1).

Iqbal, Zamir and Abbas Mirakhor (2002). 'Development of Islamic Financial Institutions and Challenges Ahead', in Archer, Simon and Karim, Rifaat Abdel (eds.) *Islamic Finance: Growth and Innovation*, London, UK: Euromoney Books.

Iqbal, Zamir (1997). 'Islamic Financial Systems', *Finance and Development (IMF)*, 34(2), June.

Iqbal, Z. (2001). 'Profit and Loss Sharing Ratios: A Holistic Approach to Corporate Finance', *International Journal of Islamic Financial Services*, 3(2), Jul–Sep.

Iqbal, Zubair and Abbas Mirakhor (1987). Islamic Banking, IMF Occasional Paper No.49, Washington: International Monetary Fund.

Iqbal, Munawar *et al.* (1999). Challenges Facing Islamic Banking, Jeddah, Saudi Arabia: IRTI, Occasional Paper No.2.

Islamic Fiqh Academy of the Organization of Islamic Conference (1989). 'Islamic Fiqh Academy Resolutions and Recommendations', Jeddah, Saudi Arabia.

Kahf, Monzer (1998). 'Asset Ijara Bonds', in Ausaf, Ahmad and Khan, Tariqullah (eds), *Islamic Financial Instruments for Public Sector Resource Mobilization*, Jeddah, Saudi Arabia: IRTI.

Kahf, Monzer (1997). 'The Use of Assets Ijārah Bonds for Bridging the Budget Gap', in Ahmad, Ausaf and Khan, Tariqullah (eds.). *Islamic Financial Instruments for Public Sector Resource Mobilization*, Jeddah, Saudi Arabia: Islamic Research and Training Institute, pp. 265–316.

Kahf, Monzer (1996). 'Distribution of Profits in Islamic Banks', *Studies in Islamic Economics*, 4(1).

Kahf, Monzer (1994). 'Time Value of Money and Discounting in Islamic Perspectives Revisited', *Review of Islamic Economics*, 3(2).

Kahf, Monzer and Khan, Tariqullah (1992). *Principles of Islamic Financing*, Jeddah, Saudi Arabia: IRTI.

Karim, Rifaat Ahmed Abdel (2001). 'International Accounting Harmonization, Banking Regulation and Islamic Banks', *The International Journal of Accounting*, 36(2), 169–193.

Karsten, I. (1982). 'Islam and Financial Intermediation', IMF Staff Papers, March, 29(1), 108–142.

Khan, Mohsin and Abbas Mirakhor (1993). 'Monetary Management in an Islamic Economy', *Journal of Islamic Banking and Finance*, 10, Jul–Sep, 42–63.

Khan, Mohsin and Mirakhor, A. (1986). 'The Framework and Practice of Islamic Banking', *Finance and Development*, September.

Khan, Mohsin S. and Mirakhor, A. (1992). 'Islam and the Economic System', *Review of Islamic Economics*, 2(1): 1–29.

Khan, M. (1987). 'Islamic Interest-Free Banking: A Theoretical Analysis', in Khan, Mohsin S. and Mirakhor, Abbas (ed.). *Theoretical Studies in Islamic Banking and Finance*, Texas, USA: The Institute of Islamic Studies, pp. 15–36.

Khan, Mohsin S. (1986). 'Islamic Interest-Free Banking: A Theoretical Analysis', IMF Staff Papers, 33(1): 1–27, March.

Khan, M.Y. (2001) 'Banking Regulations and Islamic Banks in India: Status and Issues', *International Journal of Islamic Financial Services*, 2(4), Jan–Mar.

Khan, M.F. (1999). Financial Modernisation in the Twenty-First Century and Challenges for Islamic Banking', *International Journal of Islamic Financial Services*, 1(3), Oct–Dec.

Khan, M.F. (1991). Comparative Economics of Some Islamic Financing Techniques, Research Paper No.12, Islamic Research and Training Institute, Islamic Development Bank: Jeddah, Saudi Arabia.

Khan, Tariqullah and Ahmad, Habib (2001). Risk Management: An Analysis of Issues in the Islamic Financial Industry, Jeddah, Saudi Arabia: IRTI, Occasional Paper #5.

Khan, Tariqullah (1995). 'Demand for and Supply of PLS and Mark-up Funds of Islamic Banks – Some Alternative Explanations', *Islamic Economic Studies*, 3(1), Jeddah, Saudi Arabia: IRTI.

Khan, Tariqullah and Habib, Ahmad (2001). Risk Management: An Analysis of Issues in the Islamic Financial Industry, Jeddah, Saudi Arabia: IRTI Occasional Paper #5.

Maroun, Y. (2002). 'Liquidity Management and Trade Financing', in Karim, R. Abdel and Archer, S. (eds.). *Islamic Finance: Innovation and Growth* (pp. 163–175). Euromoney Books and AAOIFI.

Mirakhor, Abbas (1995). 'Theory of an Islamic Financial System' in *Encyclopaedia of Islamic Banking*, London, UK: Institute of Islamic Banking and Finance.

Mulajawan, D., Dar, H.A. and Hall, M.J.B. (2002). 'A Capital Adequacy Framework for Islamic Banks: The Need to Reconcile Depositors' Risk Aversion with Managers' Risk Taking', Economics Research Paper, 2–13, Loughborough University.

Naughton, S.A.J. and Tahir, M.A. (1988). 'Islamic Banking and Financial Development', *Journal of Islamic Banking and Finance*, 5(2).

Nienhaus, V. (1983). 'Profitability of Islamic PLS Banks Competing with Interest Banks: Problems and Prospects', *Journal of Research in Islamic Economics*, 1(1): 37–47.

Nienhaus, V. (1986). 'Islamic Economics, Finance and Banking – Theory and Practice', *Journal of Islamic Banking and Finance*, 3(2): 36–54.

Norman, A.A. (2002). 'Imperatives for Financial Innovation for Islamic Banks', *International Journal of Islamic Financial Services*, 4(2), Oct–Dec.

Obaidullah, Mohammad (1998). 'Capital Adequacy Norms for Islamic Financial Institutions', *Islamic Economic Studies*, 5(1–2).

Obaidullah, Mohammad (1998). 'Financial Engineering with Islamic Options', *Islamic Economic Studies*, 6(1), IRTI, IDB.

Obaidullah, Mohammad (1999). 'Islamic Financial Options: Potential Tools for Risk Management', *Journal of King Abdulaziz University (Islamic Economics)*. Saudi Arabia, 11, 3–28.

Obaidullah, Mohammad (2000). 'Regulation of Stock Markets in an Islamic Economy', Proceedings of the Third International Conference on Islamic Banking and Finance, August, Loughborough University, Leicester, UK.

Obaidullah, Mohammad (2001). 'Ethics and Efficiency in Islamic Stock Markets', *International Journal of Islamic Financial Services*, 3(2), Jul–Sep.

Obaidullah, Mohammad (2001). 'Financial Contracting in Currency Markets', *International Journal of Islamic Financial Services*, 3(3), Oct–Dec.

Obaidullah, Mohammad (2002). 'Islamic Risk Management', *International Journal of Islamic Financial Services*, 3(4), Jan–Mar.

Presley, John R. and Sessions, John, G. (1993). 'Islamic Economics: The Emergence of a New Paradigm', *Journal of Economic Theory*.

Qami, I.H. (1995). 'Regulatory Control of Islamic Banks by Central Banks', in Encyclopaedia of Islamic Banking and Insurance, Institute of Islamic Banking and Insurance: London, pp. 211–215.

Rahman, Y.A. (1999). 'Islamic Instruments for Managing Liquidity', *International Journal of Islamic Financial Services*, 1(1), Apr–Jun.

Rosly, A.R. and Sanussi, Mohammed M. (1999). 'The Application of Bay-al-Inah and Bai-al-Dayn in Malaysian Islamic Bonds: An Islamic Analysis', *International Journal of Islamic Financial Services*, 1(2), Jul–Sep.

Salehabadi, A. and Aram, M. (2002). 'Islamic Justification of Derivative Instruments', *International Journal of Islamic Financial Services*, 4(3), Oct–Dec.

Sarker, M.A.A. (1999). 'Islamic Business Contracts: Agency Problems and the Theory of Islamic Firms', *International Journal of Islamic Financial Services*, 1(2), Jul–Sep.

Sarwar, A.A. (1995). 'Islamic Financial Instruments: Definition and Types', *Review of Islamic Economics*, 4(1), pp. 1–16.

Sundararajan, V., Marston, David and Shabsigh, Ghiath (1998). 'Monetary Operations and Government Debt Management under Islamic Banking', WP/98/144, Washington, DC: IMF, September.

Sundararajan, V. and Errico, L. (2002). 'Islamic Financial Institutions and Products in the Global Financial System: Key Issues in Risk Management and Challenges Ahead', IMF working paper, IMF/02/192, Washington: International Monetary Fund, November.

Udovitch, Abraham L. (1981). Bankers Without Banks: Commerce, Banking and Society in the Islamic World of the Middle Ages, Princeton Near East Paper No.30, Princeton, NJ: Princeton University Press.

Udovitch, Abraham (1970). Partnership and Profit in Early Islam, Princeton, NJ: Princeton University Press.

Uzair, Mohammad (1955). An Outline of 'Interestless Banking', Raihan Publications, Karachi.

Uzair, Mohammad (1982). 'Central Banking Operations in an Interest-Free Banking System', in Ariff, M. (ed.).

Zaher, T. and Hassan, K. (2001). 'A Comparative Literature Survey of Islamic Finance and Banking', *Financial Markets, Institutions and Instruments*, 10(4): 155–199, November.

ALSO PUBLISHED BY THE AUTHOR

Islamic Finance in a Nutshell: A Guide for Non-Specialists, 2010, John Wiley & Sons, Ltd, Chichester

Frequently Asked Questions in Islamic Finance, 2010, John Wiley & Sons, Ltd, Chichester

Introduction to Islamic Banking and Finance, 2011, John Wiley & Sons, Ltd, Chichester

The Islamic Banking and Finance Workbook: Case Questions and Answers, 2011, John Wiley & Sons, Ltd, Chichester

Islamic Capital Markets, 2009, available from the author.

Sukuk: a Definitive Guide to Islamic Structured Finance, 2008, available from the author.

Islamic Banking and Finance in the Kingdom of Bahrain, 2002, Bahrain Monetary Agency.

Financial Economics, 2001, Financial Times-Prentice Hall (translated into Chinese).

Economics for Financial Markets, 2001, Butterworth-Heinemann.

What Drives Financial Markets? 2001, Financial Times-Prentice Hall.

What Drives the Currency Markets? 2002, Financial Times-Prentice Hall.

Fed Watching: The Impact of the Fed on the World's Financial Markets, 1999, Financial Times-Prentice Hall.

The Valuation of Internet and Technology Stocks, 2002, Butterworth's-Heinemann.

The International Debt Game: a Study in International Bank Lending (co-author), 1985, Graham and Trotman.

A Businessman's Guide to the Foreign Exchange Market, 1985, Graham and Trotman.

Monetary Economics, 1985, Graham and Trotman.

Foreign Exchange Handbook,(co-author), 1985, Graham and Trotman.

Gold: An Analysis of its Role in the World Economy, 1982, Graham and Trotman.

The Finance of International Business, 1979, Graham and Trotman.

Index